When Push Comes To Shove
Volume II

Editors

Ian Clayton Ian Daley Robert Gate

Photographers

Brett Hambling

Porl Medlock

Lawrence Burrow

Michael Steele

YORKSHIRE ART CIRCUS

1995

Published by **Yorkshire Art Circus**
School Lane, Glass Houghton, Castleford
West Yorkshire, WF10 4QH
Tel: 01977-550401
Visit the *When Push Comes To Shove*
World Wide Web Site at http://www.brad.ac.uk/~cgrussel/yac/push

© Text: Yorkshire Art Circus and contributing authors
© Photographs: Brett Hambling, Porl Medlock, Lawrence Burrow, Michael Steele
© Cover photographs: Brett Hambling, Michael Steele
Typesetting: Ian Daley at Art Circus Education
Printing: Thornton and Pearson Ltd., Bradford

ISBN 0 898311 14 5
Classification: Sport/Photography

Art Circus Support Team
Jill Brown, Clare Conlon, Isabel Galan, Lorna Hey, Pam Oxley, Reini Schühle

Yorkshire Art Circus is a unique book publisher. We work to increase access to writing
and publishing and to develop new models of practice for arts in the community.
Please write for details of our full programme of workshops and our current booklist.

Yorkshire Art Circus is a registered charity No 1007443

We would like to thank the following organisations for their support:

Open Rugby, Rugby League Express, Ned Thacker at Yorkshire Television, Chris Russell at Bradford University

Contributors

Ken Arthurson	Isabel Galan	David Maxey	Garry Schofield
Dorothy Atkinson	Len Garbett	Colin McGuigan	David Scott
Gary Austin	Robert Gate	Alison Millard	George Semmence
Steven Ball	Trevor Gibbons	D A Mitchell	B Shacks
Peter Barker	Barry Glynn	Kevin Moore	John Sheard
Martin Barrass	Andy Gosling	Geoffrey Moorhouse	Rod Simpson
Neil Birch	Hillary Gray	Arnie Morgan	Henry Skrzpecki
Stephen Boothroyd	Roger Green	Lorne Mosley	Guy Smith
Phil Brennan	Allison Griffin	C E Moxon	Byron J Stogden
Gerald Brookman	D Guy	Gary Murgatroyd	Robin Surtees
Chris Burton	Margaret Haines	Bill Nelson	Patrick Tawney
Tim Butcher	Tracey Haking	Trevor Nelthorpe	Mandy Tawney
John Callaghan	Brian Hambling	Florence Nicholls	Dickie Thomas
Emma Clarke	Garry Hargreaves	John O'Neill	David Thompson
Ged Clarke	David Hinchliffe M.P.	Mike O'Neil	C Todd
Terry Clawson	Emma Hurst	Heather Parkinson	Les Tonks
Ray Connolly	Sandra Hutchinson	Dale Petty	Mike Travers
Andrew Cudbertson	Ian Jackson	Alan Plater	Neil Tunnicliffe
Ian Daley	Janet Jennings	John Pollard	Mike Ulyatt
Mick Daley	Curtis Johnstone	Brian Pratt	Russ Walker
Stuart Duffy	Reg Jukes	Rachel Pressley	Bill Watts
Diane Douglas	Martin Kelner	Margaret Ratcliffe	David Ward
Steve Edmonson	Philip Lambell	Barry Rennison	Trevor Whitaker
Hilary Ellington	Michael Latham	Danny Reuben	Michael Whitcombe
Geoff Ellis	Peter Lawrance	Bill Riley	Johnny Whiteley
John Etty	Keith Lister	Chris Russell	Revd. John Wickstead
Dave Farrar	Sir Geoffrey Lofthouse MP	Alex Service (taped interview with the	Cassie Willescroft
Phil Fearnley	R Lowe	late Frank Collier)	Chris Wilson
Trevor Foster	Peter Lush	Alex Service (taped interview with the	Nigel Winnard
Andrew Flower	Bill Lythgoe	late Alf Ellaby)	Terry Wynn MEP
Julie Flower	Phil Lyon	Martyn Sadler	Peter Young

Contents

Foreword

Johnny Whiteley And Me

I've always been a bit confused in my sporting loyalties. As a native of Jarrow I learned from birth that the greatest footballers in the history of the world were from the North East and the greatest of these was Raich Carter. But when the family moved to Hull I discovered it wasn't that simple. There was this other game called Rugby League and there were only two teams in the world: one played at the Boulevard and the other at Craven Park, rest its soul.

From memory, the first game I ever saw was Hull against Halifax at the Boulevard. It was a pretty dour affair which Hull won 4-0 with two penalties by Freddie Miller, a legendary full-back who had a racehorse named after him. There were two: Freddie M and Charlie B, after Charlie Booth, another hero of the day.

Time passed and I saw many matches, in both codes, but chose to celebrate Rugby League in a television series called Trinity Tales - about a group of supporters going to Wembley for the Cup Final. This was in 1974, by which time football had lost much of the community warmth that I recalled from early visits to Roker Park, St James Park and Boothferry Park. There were traces of poison on the terraces but what we didn't know was that Rupert M was lurking round the corner, determined to ruin everything, in pursuit of global glory and hard cash.

But let's finish with happier tales. During my Hull years I got to know many of the local Rugby League players, mainly in the context of raising money for good causes. Colin Hutton lent us Craven Park for a charity football match in aid of our newly-opened theatre, though he was a bit miffed that players like Michael Parkinson and Tom Courtenay drew a bigger crowd than the Rovers team of the period.

My finest hour was one evening in the late 1970s when Johnny Whiteley, the greatest loose-forward of our time (ask anyone in West Hull) and I were invited to a youth club on an estate in North Hull to present some Duke of Edinburgh awards. Johnny and I took turns, handing out the prizes. It was quite a contrast. Johnny, though retired, was still fit as a fiddle - tall, muscular, glowing with health - and there he stood, alongside this small, bald, wrinkled writer looking, to quote Dick Vosburgh, like something a stone crawled out from over.

Afterwards we had tea and buns with the kids. That was when it happened. A young lass of fourteen or so asked me, in total seriousness: "What team did you play for?"

© Alan Plater

London 1995

Introduction

I have been a fanatical Rugby League supporter for over sixty years and I think this qualifies me to say that the game has been the lifeblood of many northern communities. Therefore it means much more to the people who both play and watch it, than mere entertainment or a product to be consumed.

With *When Push Comes To Shove* and now *When Push Comes to Shove - Volume II,* Yorkshire Art Circus have shown the connection between sport and people far better than anything that went before. Proof of this is in the sales. *When Push Comes To Shove* is now the biggest selling Rugby League book in the world. This means that many thousands of people who didn't previously understand the game are now undoubtedly well informed.

I regret that this game has never expanded beyond its traditional boundaries, but while I recognise the game must progress, it must never do that to the disadvantage of the clubs who have made the game what it is. We must never diminish the enthusiasm of the supporters who have always been proud to be part of the running of their club, and I certainly would not want to see control being handed over to the few at the expense of the many. I welcome new finance into the game, but the spirit of the game should not be destroyed by outside financial domination. New money should benefit the supporter and club facilities, it should not be used as a market place or bargaining block for players. The cost of players must never take priority over benefits to the supporter, but there must be a balance.

Rugby League players deserve their rewards, their career is a short one. They have traditionally been local working men, who have used their talent to better themselves. My own club, Featherstone Rovers, and Castleford in my constituency, have proved that with their remarkable Wembley records. Local players, whether they be from Whitehaven or Rochdale, York or, yes, London, should be encouraged; putting local talent into action is what Rugby League does best. I have been privileged to see many great local players develop their skills over the years, I have worked alongside them and lived amongst them.

I take great comfort from the knowledge that with writers of the calibre of Ian Clayton supporting the game, this spirit will continue. The last book did more to progress the game than anything I've known - this current book will surely do the same.

Sir Geoffrey Lofthouse MP
Pontefract and Castleford
Deputy Speaker of the House of Commons

FAR FROM THE MADDING CROWD

**"No man likes to see his emotions the sport of
a merry go round of skittishness."
Thomas Hardy**

When the first *When Push Comes To Shove* was reviewed, Trevor Gibbons in *Open Rugby* said, "What if one of these books had been done in 1895, or after Rorkes Drift Test, or the great years of the 1950s?" Obviously he was suggesting that important turning points in the game should be recorded through the eyes of the fans. This centenary season of the game gives us the opportunity to do just that.

It seems apt that in this hundredth year of the game, our oldest contributor, Florence Nicholls of Hull, is also one hundred. Incidentally, our youngest, Byron Stogden, is nine, and with a name like that he should go a long way as a writer.

We are all sick and fed up about Murdoch's money, Lindsay's vision and prima donnas wanting bonus money for so-called loyalty. Do we really need any more of that bull? Here is our opportunity to forget the Super League, the power struggles and all the other nonsense and celebrate our game. I am reminded of what Richard Harris's character says in the film *This Sporting Life*, "Stars! We don't have stars in this game, just people like me." We don't have stars in this book either, just two hundred and odd writers passionate for Rugby League, people like you and me.

I am passionate about jazz, my home town and Rugby League, not necessarily in that order. I got myself all wound up a few years ago when I had a lot of my books and records ruined in a flood. I worry and fret a lot about where I live since the area went into industrial decline - I have rarely been as upset as I was during the *Murdoch's Millions* debate.

Within days of that announcement I attended a meeting at the Unity Hall in Wakefield of three hundred Rugby League fans, to try to debate a response to the Super League plan. Before the meeting I called for a pint in The Elephant and Castle pub on Westgate. It was about half past six in the evening. People who had called in for a pint on the way home were discussing the evening papers. A TV in the corner of the pool room showed *Look North* reporting the latest Super League moves. Suddenly the bloke behind the bar started shouting at me and others in the room, he was brandishing a video cassette. "If bloody Lindsay wants to know 'owt about Rugby League, he ought to watch this." The video he was holding up was a copy of *This Sporting Life*.

Now, before the cries of "traditionalist", "parochial" and "nostalgic" start, I have to stress that I do not believe a book written in 1960 and made into a film in the same decade should reflect what Rugby League is about in the 1990s. The dark smoking chimneys that form a backdrop to the film have gone, thank God.

Rugby League these days is played in far flung places as diverse as Moldova and Morocco, Fiji and France; that can only be good for the development of the game. Look at the pleasure we have had from the recent Centenary World Cup, with the chance to see such exotica on our own midden.

Nevertheless, Rugby League in this country is still basically a working class game, both from the point of view of the player and the spectator. There is a dignity to this game that has sadly gone from other mass spectator sports, just look at soccer and the state it is in. Rugby League is honourable, fair and hard by turns, but above all it is still sport - all those who desire to call it a product take note. I don't know of any other game that takes its followers through the full gamut of emotions in eighty minutes. I know of no other team sport that demands such fierce loyalty and pride from the people who watch it.

We must all hope the lessons we have learned from the World Cup in the development of the grass roots and offering a chance to the little guys are well learned. The World Cup was a brilliant celebration of Rugby League playing and watching, a million miles away from the shallow greed and stupidity we had seen in the build-up to the centenary.

But hold on a minute. Isn't all this going a bit too far? A few months ago, at another Super League debate meeting at the Civic Centre in Castleford, I found myself addressing the newly formed "Rugby League Fans United" organisation. I said at one point that we shouldn't see the selling-off of the game as a life and death matter; "Rugby League isn't the be all and end all." I was pulled up immediately by a big lad sitting in the front row of seats. "You might think that," he said, "but it's one of the things in my life that I look forward to. I've been unemployed for a long time, I go to as many matches as I can afford, I certainly can't afford the replica jerseys or to pay into the Cash-Line, but I never miss a game on the radio. It's my link to the outside when I'm stuck at home all the time." And, of course, what he said is important. What is encapsulated in that heartfelt statement says more than any of Murdoch's money talk, marketing jargon, bums on seats speak, or bottom-line balderdash ever could.

The first *When Push To Shove* organised its stories around verses from famous hymns that we'd all sung as we grew. This time we have chosen to structure with quotes from well known works of literature that seem appropriate. We have introduced new writers and photographers: Robert Gate, the most well known Rugby historian in the world; playwright Ian Daley who was the first man to put a book about rugby onto the Internet, and the photographers, Brett, Lawrence and Porl are also well established in their profession and have exhibited nationally and internationally. Award winning lensman, Michael Steele, makes up the team for this volume.

I must also thank all the contributors to this book who have shared their stories, whether it be by post, fax, tape, or in a few cases, by e-mail.

One more quote from *This Sporting Life* before we get on with the game. "By playing Rugby League he kept his head above the general level of crap and that, to me, was the main thing." Say no more!

AS YOU LIKE IT

A Rumour Went Round Central Park
Grounds For Excitement

☐ I get the feeling this takes place in a Super League future. The pieces don't quite fit. Maybe it's a dream of some sort, since it makes sense until I try to pin it down. Whatever, I'm back in the north of England after a while of being away and I'm trying to find something. The soul of Rugby League? Lost youth? Probably just myself.

Things have changed and I'm watching the slickly packaged games on television where, with all the angles covered, you don't miss a pass and the excited commentators earn their every quid. Old Trafford, Elland Road - the big occasions. The atmosphere's stirring, the seat's good, toilets fairly clean and the car park handy for a smooth getaway. It must be a superb 'product' we have here, the number of know-alls that have said so. The beer's bloody awful, but there has to be more than that why I'm left so untouched by it all. There must be something deeper why me and my game are growing apart, like when your best mate got accepted for the grammar school and it could never again be the same.

I know Rugby League is played in some desolate places. Even in my dreams it's always in monochrome shades of grey and black. It's nearly always cold, with rain and mist drifting between ramshackle stands. And the mud. Always the mud. Unlovely places, exalted by the reverence of the people who go there. It's

> "Oh good old man, how well in thee appears
> The constant service of the antique world,
> When service sweat for duty, not for need!
> Thou art not for the fashion of these times,
> Where none will sweat but for promotion,
> And having that do choke their service up
> Even with the having, it is not so with thee."
>
> **Orlando, As You Like It, Act II Scene IV**
> **William Shakespeare**

never been the size of the altar that counts, but the size of the spirit. On the other hand, it must be difficult putting a price tag on something you can't see.

So I'm back where it all began. Searching. Standing where the old dressing rooms were at Odsal. It's pretty foggy, but that's hardly unusual. Suddenly out of the gloom come the old blokes in grubby tracksuits, carrying the sponge-bucket and kit-bag. Stiff-legged and unconcerned, one is whistling a tune I feel I should know.

The goose bumps rise and once again I hear the rattle of studs on concrete, as if a bag of marbles has been dropped. Out of the mist they come, breathing hot steam, scrubbed and greased and tense. Tommy Smales, Bernard Watson, Jimmy Thompson, Frank Foster, Keith Mumby... That unmistakeable aroma of wintergreen and warm pies all around as they disappear down the famous old slope and on into the haze. The rhythmic scrunch of their boots on the gravel rolling back to me long after they've gone.

I'm transfixed. I stare into the grey blanket of fog, oblivious to the old man in flat cap and string-tied overcoat who's materialised from the pall. Startled by his sudden appearance, I greet him. "How're you going? Nasty day."

"Aye lad," he replies, "but there's worse things 'n a bit o' rough weather."

We both stare down the Odsal slope into the fog. After a while the old fella speaks again.

"You saw 'em too, eh lad?"

When people ask me who is the finest this or that I ever saw play Rugby League football, or which was the greatest that or the other, I'm usually nonplussed and never have an answer on the tip of my tongue. The reason is simply that, after half a century of watching the game, I am aware most of all that too many great players and thrilling incidents crowd in on me, none of them separated from the rest by more than a whisker. Any verdict I might give could therefore easily be monstrously unfair (I am not the sort of juryman the average prosecuting counsel hopes to have sitting out there, waiting to be impressed by his rhetoric), so I tend to clam up and mutter something about failing memory.

There is, however, one exception to this feeble response. I do recall, with remarkable clarity, the most astonishing tackle I ever witnessed; and I've seen a lot of thrillers, most usually with wingers eclipsed at the very moment they crossed the line (but still in mid-air) or were overtaken before they reached it by some defender whose previous form said he had no right even to keep pace with them, let alone catch up. Never, however, have I seen anything as breathtaking, as truly improbable, as the tackle that Cecil Mountford inflicted on Frank Whitcombe at Wigan sometime in the late forties.

Whitcombe propped in the great front-row (Whitcombe, Darlison and Smith) which steam-rollered most opponents and made Bradford Northern such a force to be reckoned with in the post-war years. He was never less than 17 stone 8 lbs, and he always looked unstoppable. Mountford, on the other hand, never made 12 stone or five and a half feet; but he was chunky and almost indestructible, and he had one of the best footballing brains in the game at the time. Of contemporary stand-offs, only Willie Horne up at Barrow and Northern's WTH Davies were really in the same class.

It was normally Mountford's partner, Tommy Bradshaw, who guarded the rear when Martin Ryan went skirmishing upfield from full-back, but on this occasion Cec found himself as the only obstacle between the line and a Frank Whitcombe who was thundering down on him with the impetus of a charging rhinoceros; a Whitcombe, moreover, who had evidently decided to crash straight through the New Zealander, who must have seemed no impediment at all.

Out came his left arm, ramrod straight, palm opened to smack Mountford straight in the face. In that instant, the stand-off had the Welshman by the wrist (it was like watching a snake strike) and, leaning back, dug his right heel into the turf with the deliberation of an anchorman in tug o'

war, but much, much more swiftly. As Mountford leaned back against this fulcrum, Whitcombe lost contact with the ground, became airborne, was swung on his own momentum through an arc by that terribly tenacious little man in cherry and white - who let go only when the flurry of arms and legs had passed overhead was was flying at right angles to the original course, and safely into touch. It had been David and Goliath before our very eyes; also a bit like seeing the hammer thrown in a Highland Games - a hammer that lay there gasping, badly shaken, for quite a while afterwards. I never saw anything like that again, not even from Mountford; maybe because, according to a rumour that later went round Central Park, Chapeltown Road had forbidden such a potentially dangerous form of defence.

☐ I spent thirty odd years as a turnstile operator at Wheldon Lane. Therefore, most of the incidents I can relate, happened in the second half of a game. I never saw a first half between the 1960s and 1990s. I'll go back then to the fifties for this one.

Cas were playing Barrow down 'the Lane' before a thin crowd. It was bitterly cold and a sprinkling of dusty snow covered the empty terraces. A biting wind swept the ground forcing the spectators to huddle together in the stands.

Barrow were awarded a penalty. Willie Horne, usually the most reliable of kickers, missed from almost underneath the posts. It was unbelievable. The players trotted back to re-start the game, but where was the ball? Not to worry, a solitary spectator, a paper 'lad' of advancing years, was clutching it to his chest.

"Kick it Joey," came the chorus from the stand. Joey waved cheerfully to the crowd and let fly with his right foot. The ball dropped to the floor and bobbled away down the steps. The boot on the other hand - if you'll pardon the expression - sailed sweetly between the sticks to the biggest cheer of the afternoon.

☐ I was involved with an amateur club who, in the early sixties, played their home games on a meadow, courtesy of the local farmer.

Pre-season training included the cutting down of the mass of thistles and nettles. The sod had to be cut and turned to make reasonable lines. Pre-match activities saw the cows being moved off the playing area. If what the cows had left was old and dried out, it could easily be lifted and thrown away like a frisbee. If however it was fresh, then this caused a real problem. Many a coal shovel was put to good use.

Before one game, the farmer had limed the field. Not to be outdone, committee, players, wives, girlfriends and supporters made a human chain from the nearby river and, with a number of buckets and other suitable receptacles, proceeded to wash away the farmer's good work.

Many a player learned his side-stepping skills here, and there was no hugging each other after a try was scored!

☐ Ronnie Jackson was a referee in the seventies and came from Halifax. One afternoon he was refereeing a big match at Odsal. In those days the dressing rooms were situated a couple of hundred yards away from the pitch at the top of the 'bowl'. This meant that at the start and end of every match the players and officials had to walk up and down the terracing, through the crowd. It was such a long journey that the half-time break had to be taken in the speedway pits.

This particular day it was an important game and a larger than usual crowd had gathered. The game was played and after the final hooter the players and officials made their way to the side of the playing field to begin the long ascent to the showers.

Now, whether it was because of the result or whether it was just because the crowd were feeling that way out, is not known, but Ronnie Jackson found his route to his clothes blocked by several hundred hostile fans. The constable charged with ensuring the referee's safety quickly realised that there was no way he could escort Mr Jackson as things stood and enlisted the help of a mounted colleague. The huge horse and rider parted the crowd instantly, like Moses with the waves, and started the climb up the terrace. The constable grabbed Ronnie Jackson and told him to follow the horse. Ronnie tucked himself in behind the horse and good progress was made, the referee suffering no more than the usual verbal ear-bashing which is part and parcel of a Rugby League match.

Then, for no apparent reason, the horse stopped and the crowd began to press around the horse and officials, sensing perhaps a real chance of expressing their anger.

Seconds later the reason for the horse stopping became clear as it lifted its tail and unloaded several pounds of steaming manure onto the unfortunate referee who was only inches away from the equine rear.

The crowd immediately burst out laughing having seen the horse give its opinion of the referee's performance more succinctly than any of their words possibly could, and humiliate him far more than any physical assault. Thus, with the tension eased and anger abated, the crowd dispersed to make their journey home, happy with the end to the afternoon's entertainment, leaving the unfortunate Ronnie, a solitary figure squelching his way to the showers.

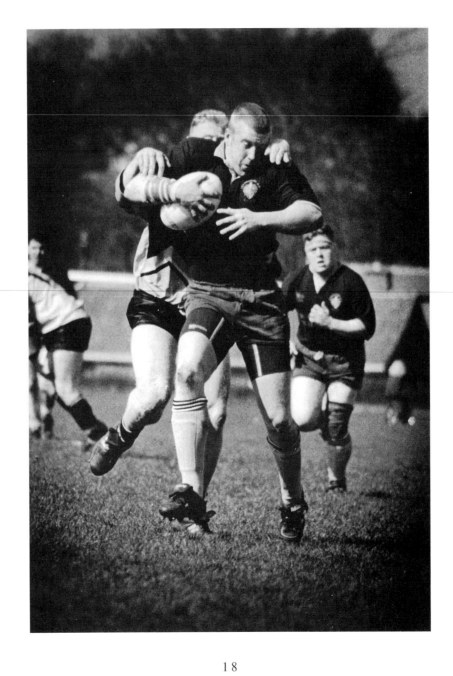

☐ I support Leigh. One really dismal, rainy afternoon, we played at Huyton. It was so awful we were fifty-fifty about going to see it. We decided very late that we might as well go and arrived there just in time for the second half. What a place! It was in the middle of a really grotty council estate, juvenile delinquency was compulsory and the tiny stand was more or less derelict. A scrum went down and I remember the steam coming off it. Then a dog trotted onto the pitch, approached the scrum, cocked its leg and peed over the Huyton loose-forward's legs. That just about summed up Rugby League at Huyton.

☐ As a Geordie, there was only one team sport I was interested in. They played it with a round ball, there were eleven on each side and the ones who mattered wore black and white stripes.

As a journalist, work had a habit of taking me to places I would never have dreamed of going to otherwise. One such occasion came along in the autumn of 1986.

I had just arrived in the North West to take up a new job in TV and was thrilled to find myself in places like Anfield and Old Trafford in the name of work. Then came the instruction to cover the first match of the Australian tour - not cricket at Old Trafford but Rugby League at Central Park.

This was going to be interesting. I'd seen the odd Challenge Cup Final on TV but never even been past a Rugby League ground, let alone inside one reporting on a game for a wide - and highly informed - audience. Still, journalists are expected to write about mass murder and a large percentage of us have never been involved in genocide.

The experience turned out to be one of the most gratifying I've ever had in the name of work. A crowd of 30,000 people gathered without a hint of that undercurrent of violence which always bubbled just below the surface at soccer grounds in those days. There were loads of women, young girls and children. Men were drinking beer on the terraces, for God's sake!

A pop band played beneath the posts, cajoling everyone to join in. Australian TV reporters followed cameras up and down the touch line. The game was being beamed live to bleary-eyed Aussies 12,000 miles away. The majority of the sporting fraternity in Britain were blissfully unaware it was taking place. They didn't know what they were missing.

Wigan were very good, the Australians were awesome, like men from another planet. The spectacle was breathtaking - fast and free-flowing, it was also tough, violent collision. The passing was at times mesmerising and the tries were brilliant. And then there were the scraps.

Fights in soccer were somehow undignified and always carried with them the extra danger of lighting some invisible blue touch paper which would set off dangerous fireworks in the crowd. Here it was completely different. Confrontation seemed inevitable when committed, powerful men collided. There's no doubt everyone enjoyed it when it flared up - players and spectators alike, but there was no invisible blue touch paper, never the faintest suggestion that violence would be mirrored on the terraces.

Afterwards, journalistic privilege took me to the corridor which had been walked by Sullivan, Egan, Boston and Ashton in the past. Now here were Meninga, Lewis, Sterling and O'Connor nursing the wounds of victory. The dressing room looked like a battlefield. God knows what Wigan's looked like. A quick interview with Brett Kenny, blood trickling down his chin: "Cut myself shaving," he volunteered.

The buzz stayed with me for days. It's there now as I look back. The job has subsequently taken me to World Cup Challenge Finals and to Wembley for the Challenge Cup and I'm always struck by the same things - friendliness on the terraces, fast and fierce competition on the pitch.

A week after Wigan, I was sent to cover a Rugby Union game - Orrell versus Bath in a John Player semi. The contrast could not have been greater. The crowd was a fraction of the one which had been at Central Park, the Bath fans were arrogant hooray Henrys, the game was dour with hardly a glimpse of skill. The only tries were pushed over by sheer, brute strength.

I left, thoroughly depressed.

☐ Some grounds stick in your mind. Blackpool's Borough Park was a great place to visit. Everybody else thought the same - let's have a day out by the sea. Consequently all the officials took their wives, girlfriends and kids for a day out to the seaside and, after the game, inundated the boardroom for hospitality. I always felt sorry for the tea ladies there. How did they know how many butties to make?

Rochdale's new ground, which they share with the soccer club, was particularly good to visit, especially if your team won. Our team thrashed them once. I remember the visiting officials gave the Hornets' whisky bottle some stick after the game. How we got back home over the M62, I'll never know. I can't remember a thing about returning home that night and I was the chauffeur!

☐ Life revolves around Cougar Park. I first started to go down there as a two year old boy on my dad's shoulders. When my dad couldn't take me, my grandad would, and he always used to stand behind the posts at the top end of the ground, as I still do today, come rain or shine. As I got a bit older, I started to notice a little girl that stood just behind me and my grandad, holding her dad's hand. A few years later we started at the same school and we began courting, most of it on the terraces at Keighley. The relationship grew and we announced our engagement. When our respective parents met at the party, we were surprised that they had known each other before. We were amazed to find out that my fiancee and I had been in the next trolley to each other in the hospital when we were born.

We are married now, with two kids. If you ever come to Cougar Park you will see me, the wife and the two kids standing behind the posts - at the top end of the ground.

☐ During the last few years I have been gathering material for a publication about Rugby League grounds. Research has involved survey work and the measurement of pitches. At one West Yorkshire ground I was puzzled by the 'twenty-five' yard lines, which measured nearly thirty yards from the goal line. After double-checking I decided to ask the groundsman to confirm if I was wrong. "Your 'twenty-five' yard line seems to measure a lot more. Do you think my tape is faulty?" I asked. He replied, "I don't know, lad. All I know is that I always mark it out twenty-five yards from the halfway line."

A few days after they played the last game at Crown Flatt, I was on my way to Wakefield Trinity's ground to carry out some survey work for my proposed book. I decided to stop off at Crown Flatt and, armed with my tape, I decided to measure the pitch before the builders came on site. I had always been intrigued by the Crown Flatt pitch, since it always appeared to be diamond shaped on ordnance survey maps. Sure enough, I was right. Dimensions taken revealed that no two lines were parallel. There was a good yard's difference between the lengths of the try lines and one touch line was nearly two yards longer than the other.

☐ I learnt about Rugby League playing Hazel in John Godber's play *Up 'n' Under*. Although I was born and brought up in Mansfield, a similar environment to the one Rugby League is played in, it's not quite on the great Rugby League corridor. There is a line in the play, "Let the battle cries be heard across our fair isle from Hull to Liverpool." That says it all really.

I was certainly encouraged to learn about the game when I was cast. I was given books to read, videos to watch, pictures to look at and taken down to live games. The spirit of the game is infectious and takes you over. During

performances, mistakes can usually be covered up or laughed off, but one night during the match sequence, I accidentally dropped the ball, and, aware that there was a rugby audience in, I didn't know what to do. It was as if they were all pointing their finger at me shouting, "Knock-on."

We Don't Play Them Rules In Hull
Characters And Humour

☐ They reckon Central Park's too central. It's only a matter of time, they say, before Wigan sell the site for development and move to an out-of-town, purpose-built, all-seater stadium. Part of a vast modern leisure complex with shops, bars, cinemas, McDonalds and ample parking facilities. I'm not looking forward to it. On match days I like to park up near Jem Lowe's chippy - "Assistant Wanted. Of smart appearance. Must be able to reckon up money without the help of an adding-up machine" - then walk down to the Charles Dickens. You can get a pint of Walker's bitter for just over a pound, pulled by a slim, black-haired girl out of one of Jack Kerouac's novels; rare butterflies tattooed all over her brown back and shoulders. You can meet your mates there, or if you're lucky, they'll be late and you just might come across one of Rugby League's charming old characters.

Last season I got talking to a seventy-six year old bloke who said he'd played for Huddersfield before the War - he told me he was centre to Lionel Cooper. What a great team that was. When the war broke out he joined the army. The sergeant said, "Where are you from, lad?"

"Wigan, sir."

"Right, you're on the rugby team."

He lost a leg in the war, which of course put paid to his playing career. It was a privilege to buy him and his wife a drink.

When I got home I consulted my reference books and discovered that Lionel Cooper only signed for Huddersfield in 1947.

☐ I know it's not a very chairman-like thing to do, but I've got this idea. I like to have a bit of fun on the tannoy when the lads go over for a try, I'll say something daft or put on an appropriate record, it might be *You Sexy Thing* for Andy Hays or *Woody Woodpecker* for Woody, but I've got this burning desire to do something bigger.

In Australia you might see them come out on to the pitch with a horse and flag - well, I want to do something like that. I'm going to get a really good cougar suit to wear, put a radio mike inside it, get one of them quad bikes, the ones that look like little tractors with the four chunky tyres, and when someone scores, I'll come flying out onto the pitch, shouting, "Another try for the Cougars," which will blast out through the tannoy. I'll then pick up the try scorer, throw him on the back and drive him back to his position. That would be so funny.

I mentioned it to one of the players and he looked at me a bit strange. I really want to do it though.

☐ Ocker, the kit man at Warrington, has to be the most famous of the Rugby League back room staff, everybody who travels there has heard of him. Leeds went up there in 1989 needing a win to take the Championship. Winning with only a few minutes to go, John Bentley mysteriously hoofed a left foot kick straight into the stand on the first tackle. From the resulting scrum, Warrington broke away and scored. Leeds lost and the Championship was gone. David Ward, the Leeds Coach, was going berserk. I took the match video into the dressing room to present it to David, he snatched it off me and threw it round the room. Bentley was cowering in the corner.

"Even the worst amateur in the lowest league in the land wouldn't have made that mistake," fumed David. It was like a morgue. The lads got changed and sloped out, trudging past Ocker, who was leaning on his swinging doors like an old cowboy. He waited for Bentley, and with what was meant as reassurance but was effectively the last nail in the coffin, said to him, "Never mind lad, you only gave away a scrum."

☐ I might be the only man in the entire history of the game to have a one hundred percent record at goal-kicking. I kicked one from one attempt.

We were playing at St Helens one day and I'd just driven the ball upfield towards their posts. I played the ball, it went out and for some reason came back again. I wasn't expecting it, but it just popped into my hands nice, so I dropped it over. Saints had a Welsh prop called Graham Rees, he looked at me and clapped. At half time, Peter Fox came to me in the dressing room and said, "Les, you've got a one hundred percent kicking record now ... bloody keep it!"

In the second half, Rees must have thought he'd try the same. He drop kicked, the ball hit the upright, came back in his hands and he charged over. As he came up he said, "Now then, that was better than yours, wasn't it?"

☐ There were always antics going on in the changing room communal baths when I was a player. When young players made it into the first team, older players would initiate them with the wintergreen. This was an ointment that was put on your body to keep it warm, always placed on the changing room table for the players to use. Experienced players would deviously go up to the new member with a large handful of wintergreen and slide it onto their private parts. Having burning balls, the victim would seek help in the bath's cool water.

The bath was the setting for all types of escapades. As I remember it, after a match at Wembley between Wigan and Hull FC in 1959, I went into the changing rooms to find Jim Drake and some other players swallow-diving off the toilet partition into the bath. While they were bombing everyone with water, the Hull directors walked in and got drowned. Jim, who was a bit of a boy, said to the chairman, "Little bit wet are we, Mr Hardacre!"

☐ I once interviewed Jack Kenny who played for Leigh in the 1930s. He told me that Leigh had a huge sunken bath in the dressing room in those days. This was at a time when most houses in Leigh didn't have baths. There might be eight players at training, but there would be thirty in the bath after it! When he played for Swinton, they had a Welsh forward who always drank four pints of Guinness before games. Jack once asked him what he did if he got caught short during the match, which was quite often, apparently. The Welsh chap said, "Oh, I just lie on the ground, boyo, and wee in me pants."

☐ A couple of my old pals, twins George and Jack Major, used to play rugby at the back end of the war - both played in the forwards. Jack played in the second row for Barrow, while George played for Featherstone, either prop or second row.

One Saturday, Jack was playing for Barrow against Warrington, who had a huge prop-forward playing for them by the name of Miller. At times he could get a little playful. During the match, Jack and Mr Miller had a little bout of fisticuffs and were called out by the ref over it; as it was near the end of the match he just gave them a warning. The next week, Warrington were playing at Featherstone, in a very rough game. Mr Miller was having a field day. I thought I saw my chance to steady him down a bit and gave him a light tap on the chin. He looked up and the first man he saw was George Major.

"I had enough bloody trouble with you last week," he said.

☐ I had a little adventure with the touch judge flag in Oxford. I was a club touch judge for the day and, whilst I shouldn't have done it, I instinctively waved the flag when one of our

players was hit on the jaw right under my nose. What I didn't know was that the offender had been given a final warning when play was on the other side, so off he went; not to the dressing room, but straight towards me! Talk about seeing your life flash in front of you. Luckily he thought better of what ever was in that murderous look of his and I survived.

The player, Frank Feighan, was a tearaway young amateur boxer who, at that time, had a habit of mixing his sports. But he later matured and found fame as a professional with Kent Invicta and Fulham, scoring BBC TV's try of the season for Kent against Castleford.

☐ I'll always remember the occasion of Paul Newlove's move from Rovers to Bradford Northern. Early on in the next season, Rovers were the visitors at Odsal and there was plenty of jovial banter going on between rival supporters. Suddenly a Northern fan announced to all and sundry that "Newlove didn't drive a Mercedes when he was at Featherstone." Quick as a flash, my mate Frank responded by informing the gentleman that "He didn't need to, there's a perfectly adequate bus service."

It's little moments like this off the field, as well as the action on it, which make me feel proud and privileged to call myself a Rugby League supporter.

☐ I've been a timekeeper since it was first introduced in 1972 in an attempt to keep up with the Australians. Down there, they have a stadium clock that counts down in full view of the fans and they chant "5-4-3..." as the clock runs out. Over here, we have a different method; each club has its own timekeeper and we sit together during the match and keep control of the clock, sounding the hooter at a mutually agreed break in play. We always blow up when the ball is on the field of play, because if you sound the hooter when it's in the stands, you'll find the kids will run off with the ball.

I don't know what television scheduling will do to timekeepers, but I remember once during a Floodlit Trophy Match, there was a telephone rigged up in our box that went straight to Eddie Waring. There had been some stoppage time so the game was going on when the programme was due to finish. Eddie Waring was on the phone going mad telling us to blow up, but we didn't. The credits were rolling up the screen and the game was still in full swing. Eddie Waring was not a happy man.

☐ Jack Senior was the timekeeper at Bradford when it first started. In his first game, he got all the signals wrong and thirteen and a half minutes after the match was supposed to finish, the referee shouted up to him, "How long left?"

Jack thought there was still another ten minutes to go. He had been stopping the clock every time the ball went out of play.

☐ Before the electric hooter was introduced to the game, we used to use a Kazoo, or Tommy Talker, as we called them. At the end of the game, we would get our Tommy Talker out and blow into the mike. It was a right laugh. In one game I was messing about with it and someone shouted, "Give us *Swannee River*," so off I went playing *Swannee River*. I'd only gone and left the mike on, hadn't I. You should have seen the look on people's faces.

☐ Just because you're a tannoy announcer, doesn't mean you can't get caught up in a game, but it can be very embarrassing if you get caught out. I once got a bit carried away by a huge up and under, it went up so high it had snow on it. The full-back was getting into position to catch it, and I lent forward and shouted, "Don't let that ball bounce." In moving forward, my elbow had caught the microphone switch and every bugger in the ground, including the full-back, shared in my excitement. Luckily he caught it on the full, luckier still, I didn't use any bad language.

☐ I turned up for my trial in a sky blue suit. It would have been 1956 and I had a 'teddy boy' jacket and 'drainpipes'. I'll always remember Keith Cotton saying, "Who the bloody hell's this here?"

Willis was still playing at the time. I remember when we played Hull - we played 'em every year at that time - Willis used to have a one-man war against their pack. They had the Drake twins, Scotty, Johnny Whiteley, all them. They used to knock seven bells of shit out of Willis, but he kept coming back. He once said to me, "If I hit them Drakes every day for the rest of my life, I still wouldn't get my own back." What he didn't know was the Drakes weren't too keen on meeting up with him either. They said, "Do you know, whatever we hit that ugly bugger with, he still keeps coming."

I kept going as well. I went from my sky blue suit to an England jersey and my proudest day when I scored at Wembley. I remember Brophy running out for Barrow, he'd cost them £13,500. I said, "We ought to play this bugger by himself, he's cost more than our thirteen."

☐ My mum doesn't know anything about Rugby League, but because I wrote the Leigh programme, the Club Secretary, John Stringer, always used to be coming round to pick up articles and what-not. John later went to work for Widnes, who signed Jonathan Davies in a blaze of publicity.

I was watching the BBC National News with my mum and all of a sudden, Jonathan Davies and John Stringer showed up on the screen. Her face lit up and she immediately asked, "Who's that with John Stringer?"

☐ In the early 1960s, Batley had an abundance of talent and competition for the hooking role. Malcolm 'Joe' Fryer, George Harwood and Bob Whiteford would have enhanced the front rows of many sides in the league and between them the rivalry was keen, but friendly. For Saturday's away game at Liverpool City, Bob Whiteford got the nod, a decision which was to lead to complications on the day.

Bob was doing National Service and needed a weekend pass in order to play, in which case he would travel independently to the ground. This was duly arranged, but as the team arrived at Knotty Ash, we were informed that, for whatever reason, the pass had been withdrawn, leaving us without a specialist hooker, and this against the veteran, but still formidable, Ike Fishwick.

The former Warrington International was one of the great ball winners in the days when own feet feeding was a practised art form, but not yet official Rugby League policy, making a good striker an essential requirement to any team. However, as usual, City were enjoying only a

moderate season and we were still not too concerned about getting a result, especially as the ever-confident Peter Fox quite happily accepted the responsibility of emergency hooker, with a promise that ball possession would be ours in abundance.

Later, as the first scrum began to form and the two front rows introduced themselves, Foxy announced to half of Merseyside that the redoubtable Ike had seen too many birthdays and that a new boy would be taking over. The craggy Fishwick remained unimpressed and, in the event, we won only two scrums and, with unlimited tackles, spent most of the afternoon chasing the ball, lucky to come away with a seven-all draw.

In the end Ike Fishwick missed out on a win bonus, but even at around forty years of age, he showed that he was still a master of his craft, at a time when wearing a number nine shirt meant more than being just a good dummy half.

☐ Refereeing can certainly be a thankless task, and referees soon learn to turn a deaf ear to the constant shouts of "off side!" or "forward pass, ref!" - especially when the perpetrator of the comment is standing at the other end of the field. However, occasionally, on the field a referee can smile to himself at some of the things said.

Here are some of the gems I've heard whilst officiating.

After winning the toss in a curtain-raiser at Headingley, the captain looked around, somewhat bemused, "There's no downhill on this pitch," he said.

During a particularly bruising encounter between Yorkshire Under 16s and the French Tourists, a Dewsbury forward turned to his colleague and mused, "I thought I hated Lancastrians till I played against this lot."

"It's my ball," shouted an enthusiastic youngster from within the melee of a collapsed scrum, "I've got my foot on it."

"We don't play them rules in Hull." Enough said!

"You're a real referee, aren't you?" I must have been wearing the shirt with the badge on that day!

"That were never a forward pass."

"Shut up, Chris. He's better than the one we had last week."

What praise could possibly be higher!

☐ We always sailed close to the wind at Mount Pleasant and this tale is a prime example of our ingenuity. We had a big weekend coming up, with Dewsbury versus Leigh on the Saturday and Batley versus Featherstone on the Sunday - televised - but we also had the Inland Revenue to pay and the weather against us. We had to be bright, so a sheet was put over the ground to combat the frost with it being such an important weekend.

At 4am on the Saturday morning, we went to check the ground; it was -4 Fahrenheit, so the assistant groundsman was sent under the sheet. He was gone for what seemed like forty minutes and when he did come up, he looked like Dan Dare, all his hair was stood up on end. He said, "It's so warm under the sheet, the grass is growing." The problem was that the thermometer was still reading -4 Fahrenheit. At 10am the pitch inspection took place; it was still freezing, but the forecast was good. Everybody was digging the ground with their heels in a last desperate attempt, so I said that I could feel warm wind on my face. I sent Dan Dare to warm the thermometer; he put it in his tea and the thermometer came back at 86 Fahrenheit. I said, "It must be a tropical wind," and the matches were played. Dewsbury played, Batley played and the Inland Revenue got paid.

☐ My father, a former player, who spent many later years supporting his beloved local team, was one of the 102,569 or so privileged fans who watched the 1954 Cup Final replay at Odsal. When I was a young lad he always used to tell me the tale about the traffic that descended on Bradford that night. Parking places were like gold dust. In fact, he told me that Warrington fans had to return to the M62 to park their vehicles and walk back to the ground! I was nearly eighteen before I realised that he was having me on.

☐ I used to play for Burtonwood Under 19s in the Warrington and District League. Our coach was an old pro who played for Rochdale Hornets - Norm Williams, I think his name was. He also played for Salford and ended up with Huyton, I think. This would be about 1970. One thing about the Under 19s League was that a lot of the players would never see nineteen again. In fact, I remember we once played St Peter and St Paul and they had a loose-forward who was a dead ringer for Barry Seabourne and had seven children, but he was still playing for Under 19s!

Quite often Burtonwood could not raise thirteen players and two subs. This particular day we were playing Langworthy and we could only raise twelve men, so Norm, who looked about seventy-six, was roped in to play loose-forward and Langworthy agreed to let him play. He had a blinder. So did I, come to that. After the game we were in the changing room and this bloke sidled up to us and told us that he was Rochdale's chief scout. He said, "That loose-forward of yours had a good game. Do you think he'd be interested in signing for Hornets?" He never even recognised he was already one of their players and had been on their books for years!

☐ Dave Hughes could have really been a contender. He was a natural born footballer but he liked a drink, and there is an unfortunate relationship between becoming a professional athlete and throwing ale down your throat like there is no tomorrow. Dave played out his career in the beer and bacca world of amateur rugby and he loved every minute of it.

We once played a pre-season friendly against the Queens club from Bradford. We all took our positions for the kick-off, the ball went flying to a Queens forward and Dave was straight up to tackle him. As the forward got to his feet, he pushed Dave rather firmly away and, almost instinctively, Dave formed a fist and smacked him in the face.

The referee called both players over. As he was walking backwards away from the rest of the players to give the two bad lads a good ticking off in private, the crowd were baiting him and as he turned to shut them up, Dave smacked his man again, the crowd roared, the ref turned round to see the Queens man flat on his back and Dave was sent off. There had only been ten seconds of play.

As this was a pre-season friendly, the referee approached Dave at half-time and told him that if he had calmed down, he could come back on and play out the second half. Dave was up for this and onto the battlefield he trotted.

Queens kicked off in the second half, straight to Dave. He gathered the ball and charged to none other than the player who he had his little tussle with in the first minute. The Queens man was as wound up as Dave and they were heading for a mighty collision, they got closer and closer, they were a yard apart and Dave threw down the ball and launched his fists in a frenzy in the now familiar and bruised face. Dave was sent straight off. The only man in the history of the game, I would guess, to be sent off twice in the same match after only being on the pitch for less than a minute in total.

☐ If you've ever watched the London Broncos, you'll know the old boy I have in mind. Barely five feet tall, and seventy if he's a day, you'll always see him decked out in his beloved London regalia - weighed down with badges of the world - chivvying and chattering to anyone who'll listen.

He's actually more Billy Wizz than Ben Gunn (he was once reprimanded for chasing female supporters round a table at Hendon FC), more your Old Kent Road than Old Trafford, and he flogs programmes like a barrowboy flogs prize apples.

One match we arrived late, just after kick-off. In we went and there he was, as usual, just inside the gate, hawking his wares. At that moment a tremendous roar went up from the stands. Programme or no programme, off we ran, straight past him, to catch the action. The faster we ran, it seemed, the louder grew the din. By the time we reached the touchline, the place was heaving with chanting, hysterical fans. All we could see were the backs of necks. Cheers rose to inevitable crescendo and melted into applause. It must've been a score, it had to be a score - but who and for which side? Whatever had happened we'd missed it.

Then behind us and some distance away, we heard what sounded like a goose being fired out of a cannon. The old Cockney Rebel himself had left his post and was thundering down the concourse towards us, whooping and slapping his ancient thigh rodeo-style. At last he reached us. Round and round and round he twizzled, to screams of, "Yes, yes, yes, yes, yes, yerrrsssss!"

It was the performance of his life. Finally he punched the air in sheer toothless delight before asking, "What 'appened?"

☐ We once went to play a friendly match in Rochdale; the proceeds of the match were for

needy children's funds. A well known lady entertainer kicked off the match and a big dinner was held after the match to which all the players were invited. The good lady gave a speech after dinner; her opening gambit was the best of the night.

She began by saying how much she had enjoyed the game and followed with, "I have enjoyed this game so much that if ever I have time to get to any of your games, I will come and kick all your balls off."

When You've Got Real Soul You Never Lose It
The Entertainment Business

☐ Wakefield Trinity supporters are used to the crowd-generated atmosphere drifting out into open space, because we have a three-sided ground. All the hubble and bubble that goes with Rugby League crowds just floats onto the pitch into the northerly winds and wafts its way out of the open end, heading off somewhere towards Doncaster. So to me, it was nothing new when the atmosphere generated for the opening ceremony of the Centenary World Cup got lost somewhere in the swirling wind and hid under the vast sea of seats that the twenty or so thousand assembled spectators could in no way try to cover.

I've always been a little bit suspicious of the pre-match entertainment at Wakefield, but I put that down to the tireless cheerleaders just not being glamorous enough. The same cannot be said of Diana Ross. She is a big noise superstar without question, but any comment on the inappropriateness of her driving round the Wembley Stadium dog track in a vintage Rolls Royce, miming to *Chain Reaction*, would be subject to serious understatement. It was all very embarrassing.

The real day's entertainment was magnificent. The entrance of the teams onto the pitch coincided with the entrance of ten to fifteen thousand supporters who had probably, and wisely, just fallen out of a pub. The atmosphere was electric and the game was full of the ups and downs and thrills and glorious skills that we came all the way from Wakefield to enjoy. It was Rugby League at its glorius best. To see the smile on Paul Newlove's face, as he crashed over for a try from an intercepted pass, was worth the ticket price alone. We'd beaten the Aussies and all went home happy.

I heard on the way back up the M1, that Diana Ross had flown in on Concord, did her spot and flew straight back to America to be with her son on his birthday. I heard that she didn't even watch the match. I wondered to myself how much it would have cost to get her for that day

and wondered how much it would cost to build a stand behind the posts at Wakefield. I'm not against pre-match entertainment, I just don't want to pay for it. I'd like to think that all my ticket money went on during-match entertainment.

☐ On the night I heard about Rupert Murdoch's plan to form a Super League and to merge different clubs, I was doing a bit of entertaining in a club just outside of Wigan. It was frequented by one or two St Helens supporters. Halfway through my act I said, "Anyone got any good ideas what we should call a team consisting of St Helens and Wigan players? Would it be 'Pies R Us' or 'Double Glazing'?" One old codger stood up, "I think they should call it 'Middleton and Woods' - that's the name of the local undertakers." Needless to say he brought the house down with laughter.

☐ Tim Heley, the former BBC Radio commentator and spectator of seventy-four years, always liked covering games at Bramely. Most dignitaries and officials are invited for a bite to eat in the boardroom, and Tim was no exception. He used to enthuse about Bee Alton's homemade Cornish pasties and coconut cake, always the centre of attraction of the bun fight after the game.

Normally when we set off for away games, we not only know the precise location of the ground, but all the pubs within a ten mile radius. You can develop a bizarre familiarity with a pub that you visit only once per year, twice if there is a cup match. This time though it was different, we were heading to a strange ground, it was unusually early and we were all wearing ties. We were confused, the oversized tickets in our pockets said VIP on them, which we could only assume meant free ale, and we were steaming down the M62 in the general direction of Old Trafford. We were, in all senses of the words, journeying off the beaten track. We spent most of the Pennines trying to work out our bearings. We knew where The Willows was, perhaps if we drove there and had a pint in the Union Tavern, someone there might know.

We spotted a bus decked out in rugby scarves and banners. The general consensus was that if we tucked in behind that we'd be alright. Several other cars had got the same idea. When the bus driver finally came off the motorway somewhere fast approaching Liverpool and turned back on himself, obviously lost, a string of cars banked that motorway roundabout with fists waving out of windows. "Well, would you bloody..." It was the caravan of lost souls.

We finally saw the big sign, 'Welcome to Old Trafford, the home of Manchester United Football Club.' This must be it. We took up our reserved, right next to the ground, privileged guests car parking spot, only this time it was kosher, we had a ticket, we didn't have to bribe the attendant.

Now to getting in. Our pencil case size tickets didn't have a gate number, but all the turnstiles did. After a couple of circuits around the ground we presumed that these special tickets must get you in through any old gate, so we waded in. We didn't realise until we came out via the thick carpeted foyer with the big glass swinging doors and quaintly suited doorman, that there was in fact a designated entrance for us. It never occurred to us that we could go through a door; to get into a ground you went through turnstiles and that's what we did, handing our top resale value VIP tickets to an extremely fortunate turnstile operator who greeted us with, what we thought a highly courteous, "Cheers lads."

We were in anyway, and all we had to do was find the room where all the VIPs go. This was naivety out of control, corporate hospitality boxes to Old Trafford are like pubs to Pontefract. They are everywhere. We didn't even have our tickets for guidance, they were probably touted somewhere up Matt Busby Way, so we just kept climbing staircases until we came to the top and stumbled into the sponsors lounge. What a place, match day programmes to pick up, glasses of wine all nicely laid out, a very tempting finger buffet, and well dressed punters standing around chattering wearing perspex name badges. It was just what we expected

"Are you on the list, gents?" We'd been rumbled by the sagging knot in our ties and general shabby appearance. You can always spot the uncomfortable suit wearers by the state of their shoes, ours were dreadfully scuffed and shamefully unpolished. The list was checked and we weren't on it. We quaffed our wines and were escorted to our rightful home, a room that resembled the best lounge of a working man's club, dark and dingy with electric pumped beer into plastic glasses that you had to pay for.

We didn't feel very important anymore, we loosened our ties an inch, unfastened our collar buttons and got stuck into the beer. We watched the Academy final, that was being played for real a mere fifty yards away from us, on the television.

Several pints down and the place started to look more inviting. People started to fall in, players' wives and the odd director and a few club backroom staff. We were relaxing and slowly began to feel at home by mixing with the others. Yes, this was the right place for us, the tempting finger buffet and free wine but a distant memory.

We'd had enough of the television and went out for some real action. We took up our seats and moaned about where they were. The view was fine, but it wasn't one we'd chosen. When we turn up at Thrum Hall or Wheldon Lane or the Watersheddings, we turn one eye to the weather, one eye to the way the team are playing and the third eye senses where the atmosphere is going to be. Choice of where to stand is important, but when denied it, the right must be reserved to moan, regardless how good the seats may be.

The rugby was magnificent, Featherstone won a hard fought battle against the big Cumbrians of Workington, and St Helens cheered all the neutrals by beating Wigan. We retired for post match drinks to the lounge and were delighted to see all the players assembled. What a place. We bought Featherstone Rovers a round, pints of bitter for the older players, bottles of Pils for the younger lads and a half a shandy for the shy one in the corner. The ties were hanging off now and the electric beer was getting smoother and more refreshing. Eventually we were asked to leave.

In tune with the high spirits of the Featherstone contingent, we decided to drive to their home town, sensing there would be some kind of party. We hit the town and it was rocking, old players and new players mixing with fans, some lying in a heap on the floor,

some climbing on the ceiling. It had been a very important day and this wasn't missed by the landlady of the Railway Hotel, whose hospitality extended to big chunky ham sandwiches. It was the first thing we'd eaten all day.

☐ Edwin Starr is an American soul singer whose fondly remembered hits of the sixties, *Stop Her On Sight*, *Headline News* and *War*, ensured he was never short of work on the chicken-in-the-basket circuit once he slipped out of the charts. The period we are talking about is from the mid-seventies until the early eighties, when the entertainment scene, especially up north, was dominated by cavernous cabaret clubs, like aircraft hangars with flock wallpaper. While the bigger clubs could shift enough Red Barrel to compete with Las Vegas for names like Tom Jones or Shirley Bassey, the humbler ones would offer a bill featuring perhaps one of the lesser lights from Granada TV's *The Comedians* and a singer you might dimly remember from the *Pick Of The Pops* of your youth.

Which is how Edwin Starr came to be playing Chorlton-cum-Hardy just before Christmas 1980 and how he became, to the best of my knowledge, the only million-selling black soul star to attend a second division match at Station Road.

The editor for whom I was writing a 'where-are-they-now' feature on Starr had suggested, as a location for the photograph, somewhere typically northern, by a canal bank with mill chimneys in the background, in front of Manchester Town Hall, something moody like that. What, I thought, could be more moody than the terraces at Swinton? And how fortunate Swinton were at home to Keighley. A trip home on expenses and, as an added bonus, a Swinton line-up including Kel Earl, a fast and delightfully eccentric prop forward who fancied himself as a centre, Green Vigo, whose greatest hits were probably more distant memories than Edwin's, but who was always good for a laugh, and the matchless Danny Wilson, who occasionally fancied playing a little that season.

Edwin, it must be said, seemed a little less thrilled than I was by the prospect of Earl, Vigo and Wilson, and similarly failed to show any enthusiasm for the ever eager waif-like scrum half Johnny Mellor, or the ultra-reliable goal-kicking of John Gorton, who never missed a shot unless it was really needed. But he wanted the publicity and he thought it might be fun. I knew more about Swinton than he did, but I did not like to disillusion him.

Although Edwin was, and still is, I believe, pretty well permanently resident here, he had not yet rid himself of the quaint American idea

that sport is somehow a branch of the entertainment industry. So when I picked him up from a travelling salesman's hotel on the Wilmslow Road that Sunday morning, he seemd convinced it was a joyous celebratory occasion at which he was to be photographed. Joy, he soon discovered, is not a word readily associated with North West Manchester on a grey Sunday morning. And I don't expect his mood improved when a fan, who had overheard us talking, asked for his autograph under the impression he was Levi Stubbs of the Four Tops.

But I had a magical afternoon. Edwin looked the business in a fur hat and coat and had a fund of brilliant stories: about how he had spotted Diana Ross at a talent contest and recommended her to Motown, about the very early days of the Jackson Five, and about some of the legends of rhythm and blues he worked with in the fifties. He told me of the shysters who ran the little labels around Detroit gobbled up by Motown and how he was sold along with a label and became a Motown artiste without even knowing it. And, glory of glories, the action on the pitch eventually began to engage the attention of the singer. It helped that Swinton's three black players, notably Danny who scored two tries, were outstanding, and I was especially pleased when my favourite at the time, Kel Earl, whom I had commended to Edwin and who was having

a quiet game, galloped over for a typical try from the halfway line swatting off defenders with one arm, while holding the ball nonchalantly under the other. As Edwin applauded Earl's try it was almost a perfect moment. Perhaps I should have returned the compliment by finding some journalistic pretext to take Earl to see Edwin Starr. I'm sure he would have enjoyed it.

The thing about Edwin Starr was that he was always great value, whether he was in the charts or not, and wherever he performed, even in distinctly second division venues. I saw him ten years later in Birmingham and he was still brilliant. When you have real soul, it seems you never lose it. Rugby League, as we Swinton fans will sadly confirm, is a different matter altogether.

In The Face Of Blizzards Without Flinching
A View From The Terraces

☐ Roy Dickenson's mother, Ivy, was a real character. Just after the 1977 Wembley Final, in which Roy had picked up a winners' medal for Leeds against Widnes, there was a memorial game at Headingley for the family of Chris Sanderson who had died while playing just a few weeks before. Leeds were playing a Great Britain side which included the Widnes winger Stuart Wright. Ivy was chirping at him all through the match. "Show us your medal Wright, show us your medal." It went on for ages, until Stuart eventually got fed up with her and shouted, "Show us bloody yours." Quick as a flash she was into her handbag and pulled out Roy's winners' medal. "Here it is," she screamed.

☐ You never think of Rugby League players as shrinking violets, but Leigh had a player who was always shooting out of the dressing room as soon as he could when they played at home. I once bumped into him as he came out and remarked, "You must shower quick." It was a silly thing to say as he was still in his playing kit and had the muck and mud still on him. He just gasped, "You don't think I'd shower with that lot, do you?" He just used to go straight home.

One of the most popular wingers at Leigh was Phil Fox, he was always chatting with the crowd. In 1985 his centre was Steve Halliwell who was after the try-scoring record for a centre. Phil hardly ever got the ball. There was this game at Runcorn and my mate, Smally, started a conversation with Phil: "Keep going, Phil," to which Phil responded, "Not a lot of point, I'll never get the ball." Late in the game Halliwell suddenly slung out a hospital pass to Phil which arrived at the same time as three burly forwards who crashed him into touch. Bloodied, shaken and muttering, he got to his feet to be greeted by a shout from Smally, "I don't know what you're complaining about. You never do anything when you do get the ball!"

☐ The day is cold, and the standard of rugby is low, but emotions are running high, and foreheads are wrinkling hot. The pitch is brown, the sky is grey, and the language is blue. But what changes? When you devote your Sunday afternoons to watching a mediocre team put on a dreary display of knock-ons and slipped tackles, you take the rough with the slightly less rough. Things seldom go as you'd like. The points steadily clock up on the scoreboard, but not underneath the name of my beloved club, Widnes RLFC. As the goals are grabbed and the tries are taken, banter becomes bitter, the chanted verses vitriolic. Tempers turn to tantrums and tethers are in short supply.

The game is over. Temperatures don't match the weather, and something must be done. No time for banners and letters to the editor of the *Times*. Something must be done. But what?

The scapegoat is on his way to the tunnel. Face to the ground, he expects the backlash from the whip of the terraces. He knows the day was a failure, and he drags his chin in the drudgery of

defeat. The crowd are booing. The target looks up as I shout. I use his name and an adjective for the way I think his boys have performed. No flowery prose here, just hard facts.

From the freedom of expression I am suddenly trapped. He stands before me. Much taller now than on the field or in the dugout. Those times at Old Trafford, Wembley and on TV, he shrank in comparison to the thousands and millions staring at him. How I cheered and supported, urged and willed. But now I am the spectacle and he is the opposition, tables are turned and I am trapped.

"What did you say?" I have no response, or if I do it won't come out. Am I stuck for words for once, or am I too scared? He's taller than me, but there's no threat of any violence. Or is there?

He glares down, looking just the same as he did in big match programmes with those out-of-date pen-pictures. He's actually human. Not someone who lives from three until half past four and then hibernates again until the next match. Like a teacher that sleeps inside her coffin from four until nine. The border between life and a rugby match has been breached.

"Nobody talks to me like that. If you say that again, I'll knock your flaming block off." Only he doesn't say flaming. I stand there, trying to look tough.

He turns and trots down the concrete steps. The steps are decaying from the past, not

framing the future, but still they do not swallow him. He jumps over the wall and returns to the stillness, and the discomfort of the changing room. I hope I have done some good. Maybe he'll carry my anger through to the dejected heaps on the wooden benches. If so, I'll have done some good. If not, then what else is there for us to do? Stop coming? I never will and neither will the others.

☐ The professional goal kickers get a lot of stick from the crowd when they are teeing up a kick, there are boos and whistles and all sorts of noises trying to put them off. If the professionals were women, then they'd be used to it. I'm a goalkicker and I get hassled when I'm practising in the park. The kids come running round, calling me names and trying to make me miss, but I put them over just to show them.

We even get hassled by the referees. Some of the men refs can be really patronising, they will stand behind me and say things like, "I'd kick it a bit to the left if I were you love." They wouldn't say that to Frano Botica would they? But you can't say anything, you've got to show some respect.

☐ Brian Gomm was the reporter for the *Leigh Journal* and also played a bit of rugby himself. Leigh played Featherstone in a cup semi-final on a Saturday and lost. Somehow the fixture list meant that the following day the two were scheduled to meet again at Featherstone. Well, Leigh could hardly raise a team. Brian went to Featherstone on his motorbike to report the game and arrived saddle-sore and bow-legged ten minutes before kick-off. He was told he was subbing for Leigh and Les Pearce, the coach, was to be the other sub. Les was past 50 at this time.

After ten minutes a Leigh man was carted off injured. Pearce growled, "Well, it's thee or me and I'm the coach, so it's thee!" To add insult to injury, Brian discovered at the first scrum he was propping against the redoubtable Billy Harris who merely said, "Now we are going to be sensible here, aren't we?" Brian ended up wishing he'd kept his crash helmet on!

☐ There is a wardrobe in deepest West Yorkshire which contains no lesser article than one regulation blue snorkel parka with orange lining and, lest we forget, a furry hood. This particular coat hangs dormant through the summer months - testimony to a winter's devotion. It has gone in search of a hearty afternoon's entertainment in all manner of stadia. It has marched proudly along Post Office Road, woefully along Wheldon Lane, hopefully through the streets of Headingley and like a

condemned prisoner towards Central Park. It has stood in the face of blizzards without flinching. Rain, snow, sleet and hail - vertical and horizontal - have been and gone, but the parka has held its ground. This worthy robe has quaffed ale in many a hostelry - pre- and post-match. It has gorged itself on a rich variety of mouth-watering delicacies - pies, pasties, burgers, chips, hot dogs, coffee, tea, soup, the works. Its pockets have been the temporary refuge for many an otherwise drenched programme, which has become acquainted with the traditional packet of extra strong mints.

But what of summer rugby? Are the parka's days numbered? Won't there be a glut of bermuda shorts, t-shirts and sun hats in a dazzling parade at the height of the season? Probably so. But when the light begins to fade, the temperature drops and you finally realise that the game has been taken over by genetically perfect thoroughbreds, have a look round. The blue snorkel parka will probably still be there, but you could well see it muttering its way towards the exit, reminiscing about how good it was when Rugby League was a game, not an exact science.

☐ I like standing on the terraces, it gives me a real buzz. All the banter and shouting and wry comments that keep you going if the game is

getting a little boring or your team is getting stuffed. There is no better revenge to conceding a try than to hear a clever put-down shouted at the linesman as he waits behind the posts for the conversion and you know that not only can he hear the comment, but also the crowd laughing at him.

Rugby fans tend to take up the same spot week to week, season to season, it's almost spiritual. You can build relationships with people based solely on where you stand. You know where the comments are going to be coming from and you learn people's personalities by what they shout out across the field. Some people may say that it's pointless shouting at the players, they can't hear you, but it's not the players you are shouting at, it's just a very unusual way of speaking to the person stood next to you.

The cold helps too. Everybody huddles together and chips and chirps away to take their minds off the creeping frostbite or the stinging rain. My favourite crowd comment was at a mid-winter game a couple of seasons ago at Craven Park. Barrow were playing Huddersfield apparently; we couldn't see more than twenty feet onto the pitch because of the thick blanket of snow belting down. We weren't bored though, our resilience showed its face as extra banter. My toes were numb, my cheeks were

burning, my lips were wrapped around a hip flask full of whisky that was being passed around to keep up our spirits when someone behind me shouted, "Well, it's not like the old days when they used to play in 'owt."

☐ The match was a re-arranged, Oldham versus Wigan cup tie in the mid-eighties; not the famous night of Oldham's great Challenge Cup victory, but still in the days when the prospect of a trip to Watersheddings on a cold winter's night, with a touch of snow in the air, was sufficient to strike fear into the hearts of Wigan's cosseted stars.

The ground was packed, even the official 'VAT registered' attendance was around 7,500. Like most of the crowd, we had been inside the ground for half an hour before kick-off and the hair on the back of my neck stood up at the anticipation of a repeat of our recent cup victory. No one took any notice of an announcement over the PA for a Mr Smith of Hindley to report to the Secretary's office, even when it was repeated twice during the first half.

By half time the Wigan machine had hit the groove, our brave resistance had been brushed aside and we were in need of a diversion to lift our gloom. It came in the form of a solitary policeman slowly making his way around the touch line with a megaphone searching for the

elusive Mr Smith. As he finally reached us at the far end of the ground, his appeal for Mr Smith went out once again and was followed by our response, "We've found your deaf aid."

☐ There we were, arriving late at Watersheddings, having lost the way to our first away game. We rushed through the now-deserted turnstiles and entered the rear of the nearest stand. Before us was a sea of Oldham supporters with only a few specks of orange and red to be seen in the distance. Being unfamiliar with both the ground and the game we could not see any way in which we could reach our fellow supporters, so we tucked our scarves under our coats and warily made our way through the opposition fans to the front of the stand, just behind the Oldham goal line.

It was proving a successful day for the Eagles and it became increasingly difficult to hide our excitement as our team repeatedly pounded towards us. During one of these bouts of excitement, an observant Oldham supporter next to us must have noticed a flash of red and orange under our coats and promptly turned to me saying, "What's up lass, thi team's winnin'. Wear thi scarf wi' pride."

We have continued to support our team with pride through thick and thin together with all the other true Rugby League supporters.

☐ I was a seaman during the latter part of the war, so I didn't get time to watch Rugby League at home. However, I was able to follow the Great Britain teams in 1954 and 1958 on their tours of Australia and New Zealand. I've been bringing my son, Paul Young, who is handicapped, since he was a boy. Hail, rain or sunshine, we never miss a game, except in the 1993-94 season when I was unable to attend for eleven games due to heart surgery.

Hull FC are a great team with a board who look after handicapped people. Paul gets a complimentary season pass every year and they allow us to come on the pitch with the car. When Mr Kershaw of York refereed he would take Paul for tea and pops - that's the great sort of people involved in Rugby League.

☐ You get the odd dickhead who wants to have a go and the insults can get a bit out of hand. Nobody loves a referee. But I'm used to it because of my job. I'm a Detective Sergeant. There has been once or twice when I've been up to somebody who's been having a go and I've said, "Look, I'm a police officer, do something about yourself or the cuffs are on and you're down to the station... so shut it!" It works.

☐ It was two brave men who set off for Leigh on a bitter November afternoon. Stranded in

East Manchester without car or central heating, the pilgrimage to see Fartown in the Regal Trophy seemed to be the best offer of entertainment for the afternoon and my new convert followed. After a bus ride into Manchester our first dilemma arose - where exactly is Leigh?

"Well, it's in Greater Manchester, so there must be a bus. I think it's near Wigan."

Enquiries on a bus destined for Wigan drew blank looks, no mention of Leigh on a passenger information board and not an inspector in sight. With the attraction of the pub growing stronger by the minute, a brainwave arrived - the Arndale bus station. A quick dash luckily found a bus about to depart for Leigh, it was ten to two at this stage.

"How long will it take?"

"Oh about an hour."

We decided to chance it.

After meandering through the grim Salford suburbs and the pleasant Lancashire countryside, a new challenge was upon us - where was the ground?

"Well, Leigh can't be that big."

The driver was from Leigh, but wasn't sure where the ground was.

"I think it's on the way back to the depot, stay on after the bus station as this is my last run."

So at ten to three, after dropping everyone else off at the bus station, we alighted at the other side of Leigh.

"I think it's down there," said the driver, pointing down a dingy side street.

Another quick dash and our hearts leapt at the sight of the orange Stones Bitter jackets of the stewards. My companion however had a more pressing concern.

"Where can we get a pint round here lads?"

"In the bar," came the bemused reply.

My football supporting friend was incredulous at the prospect of buying a pint in the ground ten minutes before kick-off, at pub prices, in a proper glass and in a warm bar. I felt glad inside at introducing someone to a whole new ball game. This was however soon to turn to embarrassment in the queue for pie and peas.

"Who's in the red and yellow?" he asked at the top of his voice.

"It's claret and gold," came the reply through gritted teeth.

☐ Apart from motor racing in my younger days, I have never been particularly interested in any sort of sport. I had however over the years watched Rugby League on TV without having much idea about what I was watching. The only thing I knew was that it seemed far more exciting than the main TV sporting diet of football.

Needing a break from the pressure of work, I decided to take myself and a somewhat reluctant family to see a live game. We duly arrived at Owlerton Stadium to watch Sheffield Eagles play Doncaster in the Jewson Cup. All I can remember is that we could see very little of the game, we did not even find out which teams were in which colours and the Eagles lost. Refusing to be beaten that easily, the family agreed to give Dad's 'latest craze' one more try and we duly arrived to watch the Eagles take on Castleford at the Don Valley Stadium. Don Valley can be quite daunting to strangers, especially as all the supporters are grouped on one side. As we were very new to the game and the ground, we just sat in the first available seats we found, amongst the Castleford supporters, as it happened. It must have been evident that we were new, as before long the Cas supporters were explaining the game to us despite knowing that we were from Sheffield.

That was three years ago. 'Dad's craze' is still going strong and we are now part of the Eagles' match day organisation. I just regret all the years I have missed, but I am reading a lot.

☐ I remember the night McDonald Bailey played his only game of Rugby League for Leigh. It was against Wigan sometime before Christmas in 1953. There were about fifteen thousand people there and it was only a friendly. Bailey was a West Indian sprinter; I think he held the world one hundred yards record at one time. It was obvious he would not make a Rugby League player, not for a while anyway. He wasn't built for it - too thin, but obviously phenomenally fast and he was about thirty-one years old. I have heard a lot of people say that he just found it too tough, but he gave it a go in that game against Wigan, he did try to tackle. How could anyone expect him to learn the ropes straightaway? They should have persevered more with the bloke.

☐ My father, Jack Holmes, was the first man to score a try for Hull FC in a match against Batley in 1895. That team did so much for Hull, yet they were the forgotten team - hardly any information existed about them at the Boulevard. All the records of the Airlies had been destroyed by a bomb during the war which hit the ground. I decided to research the team at the library using my dad's caps as reference and before you know it, the team's photo is in the paper and I had the directors here in a swarm.

I went to my first match in 1902 when I was seven and sat with a lady, holding my dad's first cap which he won when I was born. I remember once running onto the pitch to punch a player I thought had killed my dad.

We had a small pub called The Yorkshire Ale House - most players ran little pubs. Ours was near the pier where we moved when I was five. I used to love seeing the pilots off from the sand banks and got to know all the city's pubs through visits with my dad.

He won two caps, competitions galore, the most beautiful medals and a shield. When the team won the big shield in 1902, I managed to stroll out of my dad's pub through people's legs and found my way to the Paragon Station alone. When questioned by a couple among the crowd, I said, "I've come to see my dad bring the shield home," and they lifted me up to a level so I could see my dad on the balcony. Dad saw me, but never told my mother as she would have murdered me. I strolled home, between men's legs again, back to the pub and back to bed. I was so keen on Rugby League I had to do it. I followed my father in that respect, as his passion meant that mother had to look after the pub on weekends. We'd be away all day: Friday night, Saturday night and back Sunday tea-time. Mother had to change the big heavy barrels, but when we were about to take on another pub, she put her foot down saying,

"I'm not undertaking this again, looking after the pub every weekend." So we didn't take on another pub because my father loved his rugby so much.

The team were all local lads, the furthest away being Lincoln, and one player, Jack Harrison, was the only Rugby League man to win the Victoria Cross. I've met them all, even the chairman of the Northern Union who I presented the caps to - I was nearly one hundred then. I'm hundred now, as old as the game.

"Some cheered him home,
but not as crowds cheer Goal!
Only a solemn man who brought him fruits
Thanked him; and then inquired about his
soul."

Wilfred Owen

48

GREAT EXPECTATIONS

I'll Never Forget Him As Long As I Live
Heroes, Heroines and Villains

☐ Harry's dead now. I miss him. He thought he'd failed if he hadn't a snippet of gossip to impart every time he saw me. He even watched them train - hamstrings and all.

I worried about him. Always thought he was a potential target for muggers. He sold programmes for years, sitting at a table with an old tin box full of money temptingly visible. I worried more as he grew more frail and his eyesight failed. It would have been so easy. And yet, in another way, I always thought Rugby League fans wouldn't do that. And they didn't. Not even 'away' fans.

All players were gods to Harry. The club sent flowers and a basket of fruit when he was ill. Harry never, never criticised any player, but he did once remark, wistfully, that he thought his hero might have visited him in hospital.

His scarf draped the coffin which was bedecked with flowers in club colours. The club was well represented - directors, officials, past players, but no current players. And not his hero.

Someone still sells programmes from Harry's pitch, but we buy ours from John now. John went to Harry's funeral.

☐ My first Rugby League hero was Swinton's Danny Wilson. At either centre or stand-off he was a superb player, who could do just about

> I must not leave it to be supposed that we were ever a great house, or that we made mints of money. We were not in a grand way of business, but we had a very good name and worked for our profits and did very well.
>
> **Philip Pirrip, Great Expectations
> Charles Dickens**

anything with a rugby ball.

His arrival at Swinton was made all the more exciting for me, because he lived next-door-but-one to my Nana, in neighbouring Pendlebury. I would occasionally catch a glimpse of him there, but you could never fail to see his two children, Ryan and Rhodri, who appeared to play football in the street morning, noon and night. Ryan of course became known as Ryan Giggs, no less, who took his father's rare

football talent and later his mother's maiden name.

In the early 1980s Wilson was playing so well for Swinton and Wales that some of the big clubs became interested in signing him. At one time it was rumoured that Hull FC had offered Swinton £60,000 for Wilson's signature. I told my Nana this news. Not being of a rugby mind, she thought I meant someone had offered £60,000 for Wilson's house. She commented how grossly over-priced this figure seemed to her, because the garage needed repair. The big deal to a First Division club never did materialise for Danny. Maybe £60,000 was indeed too much money.

Wilson's first game for Swinton was in the 'A' team as 'A Chinaman', in order to out-fox the Rugby Union authorities back home in Cardiff. He finished his playing career at Chorley Borough with 'most disappearances' according to the honours profile in the club programme. What happened in between was a roller coaster ride from the sheer brilliant to the unpredictable. It is interesting to see how Manchester United have cosseted Ryan Giggs. Swinton could never have done the same for his

father: he was far too much of an individualist, both on and off the pitch. However, one simple fact remains true for me and many other Swinton supporters. With the possible exception of Les Holliday, Danny Wilson is the finest Swinton player since the halcyon days of Buckley, Gowers and Stopford in the 1960s.

☐ Ellery Hanley is the master of energy conservation. I once saw him almost single-handedly destroy Castleford at Wheldon Lane one Boxing Day. The Cas faithful were screaming at their team to nail him, but they just couldn't put their hands on him. I was chatting to a discontented John Joyner in the bar afterwards and he was shaking his head saying, "He was only one inch away, always one inch." If you ever watch Ellery make one of his runs, you will see what he means. He has got the perfect balance; he will zig and zag, with one eye on the tryline and one eye on the hapless player in pursuit. If he is being chased by a big prop, he will keep one inch in front of him and equally if he is being chased by someone like Martin Offiah, he will be the same one inch away. He never uses more energy than he has to. There will always be a little extra in reserve, just in case he might need it.

There isn't a nicer man in the game than Ellery. He gets a rum deal from the press, and

opposition spectators queue up to shout abuse at him, but he really is a gentleman. He brings his mum up to the ground and you never hear him swear, it's always "Flipping this and flipping that." He also appears to be very naive. When he was Great Britain Coach, we were teasing him about Henry Paul, the Kiwi full back, saying how we thought he was better than his British counterpart, Alan Tait. Ellery was surprised: "Oh flipping heck, do you think so, oh flip, no."

It's a little known fact that Ellery can't function without his pre-match oranges. We never knew how serious he was about his oranges until one Sunday we turned up at Sheffield realising we'd forgotten them. He sent us out, saying he really couldn't play without oranges, and we were driving all round Attercliffe trying to find a shop that had some. Oranges are not the easiest things to find on a Sunday. One day in Doncaster, we had forgotten the oranges again but fruit is harder to get hold of in Doncaster than Sheffield and we couldn't find any, anywhere. We plucked up courage to go into the dressing room to give him the bad news, fearing the worst. But Ellery took it well, and in a resigned tone said, "Ok, can you get me a bottle of lucozade and a Marathon?"

☐ Have you ever tried getting hold of a Wigan player? You ring the club. A girl answers and

puts you through to the 'phone in the players' tunnel'. You try and try but no one answers. You try again. An Academy player answers and tells you the first team will be back from training at 2.15.

You ring again at 2.20. The girl from the office answers and you're embarrassed 'cos you know she's run from the office. They haven't arrived yet. You ring at 2.30 from a call box. You've missed him. He's gone home.

You ring the office again.

"Hello, Wigan Rugby League," says a voice you recognise.

"Is that Joe?"

"It is, how are you?"

"I'm fine. I'm wanting to contact ..."

"I'll give you his number but you didn't get it from me. OK? Nice to speak to you."

"I'm sorry, I didn't quite hear all the number, can you say it again?"

"I've closed the book now", says Joe, exasperated. "Wait a minute. Are you ready?"

(You're dithering, but you're ready.)

"I do wish they'd make their mess somewhere else", says the BT cleaner, cheerfully - pointing to the enormous pool of blood on the telephone kiosk floor that he's patiently waiting to mop up. You're so wrapped up in your Wigan quest you don't give this a second thought, until much later. Was there a body?

Just for a moment you believe in Rugby League again. In what other sport would an international superstar - in any circumstances - answer the club phone?

☐ Wakefield Panthers are unbeatable, you've almost lost the game before you get on the pitch. It's not just the reputation that winds you up, but the matching tracksuits. I think that's the major difference between men's and women's rugby, there isn't much trouble, but when it goes, it goes. The wind-ups last much longer in our game, I think we take things more personally than men.

☐ During the week before the 1935 Cup Final between Castleford and Huddersfield, a Castleford player was given a little nanny goat as the club mascot. He took it to the ground on the Tuesday training session and said to Billy Rhodes, "Look after it Billy." Going down on the Thursday night, he said to Billy, "Little Nanny alright Billy?"

"Aye," said Billy, licking his lips, "It was smashing."

☐ The fashionable hairstyle in the early 1970s was the 'feather' cut, a sort of punk-style spiky front and long strands at the back. Being something of a traditional 'short back and sides'

man, Uncle Dick loathed anything of this nature and took an instant dislike to anyone who sported such a ridiculous haircut. As the young Rovers' centre, Neil Tuffs fell into this category. It was Uncle Dick's firm belief that he should not be in the team and, refusing to use his correct name, he referred to him as "him wi' t'head like an hen's arse!"

Picture the scene then if you will: a vital league title decider at the Willows. The match is well into injury time and Featherstone have just scored a try right in the corner to make the score 17 - 16 to Salford. With the regular goalkicker, Harold Box, injured, it was up to young Neil Tuffs to attempt the near impossible conversion. The rest of course is history: the ball sailed between the posts, the whistle blew, the championship was won and those in blue and white went berserk.

"What about that then, Uncle Dick? What about Neil Tuffs now, eh?"

I rejoiced, leaping up and down. His reply was full of repentant praise for the young man he had so blatantly wronged:

"Aye ... well ... he wants to get his bloody hair cut though!"

There aren't too many Uncle Dicks around any more. Rugby League grounds are poorer places without them. I still miss him, especially on Sundays.

☐ It made its debut at Wembley in 1987. I had a bona fide ticket for the Press Box. I still have it. Intact. I didn't need it. The Magic Coat opened all doors. No-one challenges the Magic Coat.

It wasn't expensive; a simple Debenhams long cream wool number with slightly padded shoulders. Add a clutch handbag, high heeled sandals and a power hair-do and you're in.

Sadly, eight years later, it's still my 'best' coat. So I brought it out for my television debut. High heeled suede shoes this time, as I'd gone to the studio straight from work. Same clutch bag though. We had been invited by Yorkshire Television to debate the Rugby League future.

Sitting alone, quietly, in a corner, the patronising voice of a club director at an adjoining table enquired, "Have you been stood up, love?" followed by the predictably chauvinistic, "You're not here for the rugby debate are you?" Still, it was my own fault. I asked for it, not circulating, sitting like a wallflower with a strained expression.

It was hot under the studio lights so I rolled the Magic Coat up on the floor in front of me. The TV presenter had the final make-up touches brushed on right up to the moment of recording. Would I get the much needed make-up treatment? No. Only the bald pates received a perfunctory dusting down.

The highlight of the evening came when Yorkshire TV's supremely professional presenter, Christa Ackroyd, played a short video message from the Chief Executive who, she said, couldn't be with us because of a prior engagement in London. Maurice said fans had been asked to support re-structuring of the game which involved "little change."

As drinkies in the boardroom after the recording inevitably led to a further wallflowering, I left the studios. 8.04 p.m. I quickly calculated that I could just catch the second half at Headingley and drove away.

Now then, how to find a parking spot and how to gain admission without my season ticket or any money?

Magic Coat to the rescue. I simply drove up to the main gate which the steward opened without a word and I drove in, parking behind the cricket pavilion. Tottered on the high heels to my usual seat in nice time for the second half.

I suddenly decided to test how far I could get with the Magic Coat. I followed a group of well dressed, well heeled individuals through a door. They all showed their passes. I just smiled and let the Magic Coat do the talking.

Up the stairs and into the Taverners; right to the top and past the last line of security into the Director's Lounge. Passes were shown again. The Magic Coat just smiled.

A very elite gathering. Having achieved my object I squared my shoulders; held my head high and beat a hasty but dignified retreat. Not, however, before I had heard Maurice Lindsay enquire of his understudy, "How did it go? The usual...?"

The security guard held the door open for the Magic Coat. "Good night, madam."

☐ We had a hooker at Saints called Eric Hughes. I remember he was once in the bar at the supporters' club before a game with Leeds. He was going on and on about a scar he had on his face, which he reckoned had been given him by Bob Haigh, the Leeds test loose-forward. Anyway, Eric was going to get his own back. When the game began, the two teams lined up normally. Saints had the kick-off and Eric obviously had it in mind to get Bob from the kick-off. He must have had it in mind and nothing was going to stop him, because when Saints kicked-off they kicked-off to the wrong side of the field - to the three-quarters, not the forwards. So the ball never went near Bob Haigh. Although the ball was kicked in the opposite direction completely, Bob Haigh was spotted spark-out, lying in a pool of blood and carted off after about twenty-six seconds. No one said anything, but I reckon I know what happened. Eric had got his own back!

☐ They loved Alex Murphy at Leigh. Opposing fans hated him though. That's how it always is with players like him. If he's in your team he's great. If he isn't, you hate him.

I remember a game at Leigh. It was a right mudbath. The other team - I can't even remember who it was - was penalised three yards inside their own half. The referee scraped a line with his boot in the mud where the penalty was supposed to be taken from and then walked forward fifteen yards to ballock the guilty player. Alex picked up the ball behind him and crept forward and scraped another line about ten yards further on, then went back and got rid of the ref's line. When the ref turned round, Alex pointed to the line and instead of having to kick to touch, Leigh were able to have a shot at goal.

Well, the opposing fans went mad, but their row was smothered by the laughter and catcalls from the Leigh followers. It was hilarious. He were a beggar, were Alex.

☐ My idol was, and always will be, Eddie Waring. I have had an exciting life, but nothing will compare to the time I shook his hand at a charity game at Ripon Rugby Union Club. I also never forget the time he cruised past by Dad's car on the way back from a game at Fartown and the famous man waved at us from the luxury of his Jaguar.

☐ I had a photo took with Brendon Tuuta which is my favourite. He asked my mam to wait while he knelt down so that he was the same height as me. Then he wished me "Happy Birthday." It was on the same day as the Blue 'n' Whites Christmas party and all the players were there.

☐ I'm a rugby union man I suppose, but for the last couple of seasons I've become interested in what is going on at Cougar Park. I find league more exciting on a week to week basis than its rival code. I'm almost totally converted when I see the speed and athleticism of league, but then my union blood starts flowing again everytime the forwards huddle together in that thing they dare to call a scrum.

I should have Rugby League blood in me really, my grandad was Frank Whitcomb, the first player to win the Lance Todd trophy on a losing side. He was one of the all-time greats. He died in his forties so I was denied the chance to get to know him. I can piece bits together about him from what's been passed down through the family and looking through record books, and we have a little bit of film of him going over for a try, which I think was taken on tour. One thing I do know for certain is that he sailed out to Australia for the 1948 tour, on the aircraft carrier HMS Indomitable. I know that

because I've got the pennant hanging on my bedroom wall.

☐ I was never remotely talented enough to play Rugby League at professional level, but as an enthusiastic member of the village Under 17s, I played both with and against quite a few youths who went on to enjoy successful senior careers.

One particular game in my not so glittering portfolio sticks firmly in my mind, even after all these years. We were due to play Castleford Under 17s on the Wheldon Road training ground and our team were viewing the contest with some trepidation. At the time, the Cas team boasted a couple of ferocious prop-forwards who were sixteen going on thirty-five. Apparently one of them had been shaving since he was twelve and it was common knowledge that these two juggernauts took opposing teams apart limb by limb.

The match was played on a Sunday afternoon in November and it had been raining since the previous Thursday. The pitch made Odsal look like Sydney Cricket Ground and we gingerly stepped out to meet our fate. The whole game was an absolute farce. Twenty-five of the twenty-six players simply could not keep their feet. The violent efforts of Cas' dirty duo were completely nullified by the mud. Everytime they tried to connect with a haymaker, they simply

lost their balance and fell in the morass. Fair play to them, however, they kept trying to the bitter end, but by then we had other things on our minds, like the relentless accumulation of Castleford points.

The one man on the field who seemed totally oblivious to the conditions underfoot was the Castleford stand-off half. A small stocky youth, he seemed to simply skate over the mud whilst we mere mortals slipped and slithered in his wake. Cas beat us by forty-odd points and the stocky little lad scored six tries.

I have long since forgotten the names of the ferocious prop-forwards, but not the little stand-off who totally destroyed us that afternoon with his blinding skill and pace. I will never forget his name for as long as I live. It was Roger Millward.

☐ During the late sixties and early seventies Wakefield Trinity developed the bad habit of spending good money on some rather ordinary players from Rugby Union. Perhaps the most spectacular failure was Brian West, an England International lamp-post, who was despatched back South after a very short time.

One of these moderate acquisitions was a local union product called John 'Dan' Archer, a winger, as I recall, from Wakefield RUFC. Some of us die-hard anti-RU types on the terraces at Belle Vue used to regularly give him some real stick with references to Doris, Walter Gabriel and the rest.

At the time I was hooking for Walnut Warriors in the Sunday Amateur League. In one particular match against Pontefract Labour Club I got a good ball on the burst and made a lengthy run up the touchline. I was hit by a tackle from their loose-forward the like of which I've never experienced before or since. I was out for the count and when I came round among a group of concerned spectators I became aware of one of them peering down at me with the very broadest of grins.

It was 'Dan' Archer. He said absolutely nothing but I knew full well exactly what he was thinking!

☐ In almost fifty years of existence, Batley Boys Club has provided the game with many professional players. However, in the early days, because of the poor facilities available, lads had to be rugby mad to take up and continue playing the game.

The changing rooms were old converted stables in Field Lane, which meant a ten minute trek up cobbled streets to the pitch situated behind the long stand at Mount Pleasant. It didn't take many of those journeys for the old style leather studs to make the presence felt on

the wrong side of the boot soles! And after the game there were no baths or showers. It was togs off, clothes on and home. Some of us didn't have baths or showers at home either.

The football pitch itself was something of a deterrent, with a steep banking side sloping away only feet from one touchline. Cinders covered a part of the ground and most of us tried to avoid that particular area. Barry Hirst played in the second row and was always willing to take the ball up on that inhospitable surface. His knees bore the scars, but he never failed to respond to the call of, "Give it to Barry."

Barry Hirst never made it to the professional ranks, but his attitude epitomised an essential part of Rugby League's character. He combined honesty and endeavour with a heart as big as a bucket.

☐ My grandad was older than the Northern Union. He had been born in 1892 and before the turn of the century, he was watching Hull FC at the Boulevard. How could he know he was starting a family tradition that continues today? Before the Elland Road glory of 1982, he was the only person I knew who had seen Hull win the Challenge Cup because he had been there in 1914 at Halifax, when Wakefield were beaten 6-0. When I found this out I regarded Grandad with a new sense of awe; I knew he was old with

a name like Herbert, but this was something else, living history.

It was in the late seventies that I was regarded as old enough to sit in company with Grandad, while Mum went on the shopping trip. It was then that Herbert became not only Grandad, but my own H G Wells, allowing me to time-travel. Older people can slip into a world where 1914 is yesterday, even if they do not know what day it is. As I sat there on the settee, we journeyed back and Grandad would name complete pre-war Hull teams, asking me to help him fill in that centre's name he just couldn't recall, projecting his memory onto my small store.

That 1913-14 season, when the cup was won, had been Hull's best season to date in the Northern Union and most of the names tripped off Herbert's tongue - Bert Gilbert, Beasty, Jimmy Devereux, Alf Francis and of course Jack Harrison and Billy Batten.

Jack Harrison's try scoring record still stands, it was the club's fiftieth season in existence, but of course far darker shadows were being cast over the continent. At the end of that season, twenty-four Hull players joined up. The war to end all wars was beginning. My grandad joined the East Yorkshire Pals too, but he was never to speak of those experiences, dwelling instead on the golden exploits of the heroes of his youth ... and I went there with him.

The Joke About Watford Gap
Down Wembley Way

☐ Every Sunday without fail he would arrive at our house at midday, have his Sunday dinner, smoke his pipe for ten minutes and then fall asleep in the armchair. At 2.45 pm precisely it was my job to wake him from his slumbers in preparation for the short journey to the Holy Shrine at Post Office Road.

To my knowledge, Uncle Dick ventured further than the county of Lancashire on only five occasions: four times to watch Featherstone Rovers at Wembley and once when I persuaded him to accompany me to Whitehaven for a first round Challenge Cup tie. On the latter occasion, imagine the uproar of laughter on the coach as it meandered through the awesome Lake District mountains, when Uncle Dick announced to all and sundry, "By 'eck, they've made a grand job of re-seeding them pit stacks!"

The journeys to Wembley with Uncle Dick were naturally entertaining. Not for him the subtle jokes about needing passports at Watford Gap, but a humour which again displayed his total innocence and delightful naivety. Much was the consternation on the afternoon of Friday 11th May 1973, as my father's Vauxhall Viva coughed and spluttered to a halt just before Leicester Forest Services. Could it be fixed for us to reach the hotel in Watford in time for the evening meal, demanded my mother. Could it be fixed in time for us to make the kick-off the following day, demanded yours truly. As my father tinkered and cursed under the bonnet, Uncle Dick remained resident in the back seat, where he lit his pipe, smoked for ten minutes, then pulled his flat cap over his eyes and promptly fell asleep.

He woke up some hours later as we eventually arrived at the hotel: my mother was flustered, my father was covered in oil and I was half-starved. We entered the hotel and immediately headed for the dining room where we hoped to salvage what was left, if anything, of the evening meal. As we sat down, Uncle Dick decided it was high time to visit the 'Gents'.

"He's a martyr to that bladder of his," was my mother's constant Thora Hird-like euphemism.

In Uncle Dick's absence, the waitress informed us of the meagre fare on offer; we placed our order and she scuttled off to the kitchen. The arrival two minutes later of the wine waiter unfortunately coincided with the return of Uncle Dick, relieved and refreshed, but ignorant of the fact that the food had been ordered. Imagine therefore my mother's terrible embarrassment when the unsuspecting wine waiter thrust a wine list in front of Uncle Dick and made the polite request, "Would sir like to select a bottle of wine?"

Uncle Dick blinked twice rapidly, banged his pipe on the table, and replied, "Nay lad, it's summat to bloody ate we want!"

☐ Drinking in the Metropolis, just off Baker Street, feeling like an outsider: Northern accents, gallons of bitter beer, loads of strange team strips. It's only the ranks of Aussies that let me know I'm in London. My second Rugby League experience beckoned. From Widnes to Wembley in two games, pretty good going.

England versus Australia in the opening game of the Centenary World Cup. A fantastic occasion, despite the marketing, especially given that we could actually beat the Antipodeans at something. Suitably oiled we took our seats, knees firmly pressed against chin (good old Wembley) having tactically avoided Diana Ross, best move of the afternoon by all accounts. The worst move being our seats in the Aussie end. No matter.

A crowd large enough to provide atmosphere and a match to stir passion in a League virgin. I shouted my scripted lines, "That were forrad," "Gettem on side!" Triffic.

The match was finely balanced and virtually all square at half time. Enter the Fiji Dance Troupe, striking fear into the groundsmen who

had one eye on the divets they were sent to replace, and one eye on the spears that they had to avoid. Marvellous.

The hooter signalled the start of the second half, the game's advantage flashed between the Whites and the Greens. More entertaining than chase the egg at Twickers, we enthused. Suddenly there he was, Newlove, my new-found hero, grinning over the line to score the winning try. All quiet on the Aussie front. All noisy in our island of white.

The Man of the Match announcement signalled the beginning of the end, a fact which the sea of green and yellow around me had no choice but to accept. The whole match was over in what seemed like less than a minute.

"You're nothing but a bunch of bar staff," I shouted at the depressed green face-painted throngs.

"I'm off to Earls Court to reclaim the streets," I declared. It was brilliant.

"See ya at the final then, Pom."

"It's a distinct possibility. Pint of Theakstons please, Aussie."

☐ This is a story about a little pub side from a village, beating all the odds to reach their Wembley.

It's nine o clock on the morning of Saturday 16 April 1985 and we're on our way. It's the third round of the BARLA National Cup. My team, The Jubilee, are taking on the might of Cumbria, Wath Brow Hornets, who are being tipped to lift the coveted trophy. Twelve of our team worked at Ackton Hall Colliery, we had just completed a year on strike in our fight to save jobs. What with all that picketing, running from the police, trudging over fields and coal picking, we were as fit as the proverbial 'butcher's dog'. We had beaten Wigan St Cuthberts and Bradford Top House in the two previous rounds, so we knew we had a good chance against these. Confidence was sky high and comradeship second to none. The fifteen that turned out that day did Featherstone proud. We won 30-14 in a classic hard amateur game. Our coach, ex Fev and Hull star, Vince Farrar, told us to enjoy the moment, the hard work was still to come.

By, did he mean it. Training the next two weeks was harder than ever. Another tough away game, that Thatto Heath home of the great Alex Murphy. We overcame a big team that day - 16-6, to earn a home game against the holders of the cup, Dudley Hill of Bradford, in the quarter final. More tough training and the day of the big game came. The Purston Park was chock-a-block when we ran out, what an atmosphere! In end to end rugby we overcame the holders 18-15.

Back at the 'Jube' we all huddled round the radio to listen to the draw. Out it came to a great roar, "Jubilee versus Egremont". We got the draw we wanted, a home tie in the semi final. That was three weeks away. Vince stepped up the training again; we were still playing league and local cup games as well, so we were always on our toes and keeping match fit.

Nearly half of Featherstone must have turned out that day, there wasn't a space anywhere in the park. The crowd was huge and, believe it or not, it snowed! The beginning of May and we had a snow storm! In what was a really tough game, we again came out on top, 14-8. We were in the final! Up to that year the final had always been played at Blackpool, this year it was Headingley. We were going to miss a weekend at the seaside, but who cares.

Celebrations after that semi final win went on for days. At the pit everyone was on about it and the final couldn't come soon enough for me. It was really nerve-racking, everyone stopping you and talking about our chances, but it was nice though, because when you thought about it, here was the amateurs' equivalent to playing at Wembley. Vince did us proud with the training that year. I don't think he got the praise he deserved during that cup run.

We were ready. A light training run Saturday morning, followed by lunch someone had put on

for us and an early night. Sunday morning at eleven o'clock and we all start to congregate at the 'Jube'. Photos are taken, we look smart in our new jumpers and ties, and trousers made for us by the lasses at Grantwear. Coaches were already leaving Featherstone full of supporters and ale. What a feeling it was watching them all go to watch us. Then it was our turn to board the coach and set off for the biggest game of our lives.

We got into the changing rooms - ours was the one that Leeds RLFC used, it was huge - and changed into our new strip. Everyone was edgy to say the least, I was sick in the toilet ten minutes before we went out. We lined up behind our chairman, Mr Stan Nicholson, and our coaches, Vince Farrar and Tiddler Simpson. The ref blew and we were off.

In a match that seemed to last two minutes, we played some lovely rugby in front of nearly five thousand fans. We would have beaten anybody that day. Everything came right; from number one to number fifteen, we all did our jobs and won the cup for the 'Jube'. The score was 26-10. The job was done and it was back to Fev for what can only be described as the biggest piss-up the 'Jube' has ever known. What a night! To me it showed what the amateur game of Rugby League is all about, a good hard game, friendship and a good social life.

Two years previously, Featherstone Rovers had a famous win at Wembley with a team of miners from the same pit. Anything they can do...

☐ This is a cautionary tale. Pay attention. It could happen to you.

The best way to enjoy Wembley is to arrive at least three hours before kick-off. You don't want to be rushing at the last minute do you? Park close by. Go for a stroll. Buy your programme and take it back to the car. Spot the celebrities arriving. Wonder why touts look so scruffy. Weigh up the weather so that you are wearing the right clothes. You can always return to the car for an extra jumper.

About half an hour before kick-off, you enter the stadium. Wander to the loo. Pay £1.50 for a bag of Opal Fruits and vow never, ever to forget sweets again.

OK so far? Fine. Twenty minutes to kick-off.

Ascend the steps and realise, when you can't see the nearest goal post or make out which enormous inflatable is the kangaroo and which is the lion, that you have forgotten your spectacles.

Instant decisions now. Engage brain into overdrive. Run up and down the stairs to find a steward. Those with orange bibs are showing people to seats. You explain your full story and

orange bib tells you to find a red bib. (Bear in mind here that all Salford shirts look like red bibs - when you haven't got your glasses on.) Red bib tells you he can't do anything and you must try and find a white bib, ie a supervisor. You tell your full tale again to white bib who suggests you find the security officer.

You find the security office and there is a long queue because you are not the only idiot trying to get out and hoping to get back in.

Your ticket is stamped and initialled.

You run back to the car in pouring rain (in your first-time-on new trainers). Naturally, the milling hordes are all going up Wembley way; you're the only one going down and the car suddenly doesn't seem all that near. You have to rummage through all the clothes, empties, programmes, papers and rubbish stuffed in the boot to find your specs. You run back to the stadium but you've lost your bearings and can't remember which door you came out of, which is important - that's the only way you will get back in.

You find it and there's a queue and it's really raining now. You run round the entire circumference of the stadium for the umpteenth time to find your aisle. They're playing the anthems. You run to your seat. They kick-off. You can't see a thing; you're sweating and your glasses are steamed up. Piece of cake.

☐ We usually went shopping as a family on a Saturday afternoon, but my wife had tripped and badly sprained her ankle during the week, so we were watching *Grandstand* on television when details of the 'Top Try of the Season' competition were announced.

"Come on Nick, we'll enter this," I said to my ten year old son. We had to choose the best three tries and agreed on the first two, but had different ideas about the number three try, so we posted off separate entries the next day.

Karen Williamson of BBC TV rang the following week to let Nick know his selection had matched Alex Murphy's opinion! The prize was rail and match tickets for the 1985 Wembley Cup Final, between our team Hull FC and Wigan. We had actually already booked on a coach trip, but the BBC were very good and offered to give Nick the cash equivalent of the cost of the rail tickets. We sold our match tickets, as the BBC's were nearer to the Royal Box.

We were told to report to the BBC mobile studios at Wembley at 12.30 pm on the day. The *Hull Daily Mail* had earlier that week sent a photographer to Nick's school and a picture appeared on the front page with his mates lifting him high in the air.

Come the Saturday, we left Hull at 8.00 am and arrived at Wembley in good time. When we presented ourselves at the BBC's studios, the assistant asked me if Nick would like to do a live interview with Des Lynam. Would he! Nick met Bob Wilson and Ray French and, although I was worried about Nick drying up when Des Lynam interviewed him, I needn't have worried; he spoke very well, wearing his black and white scarf. The BBC had even rung my wife at home and told her we would be live and she had to ask our next door neighbour to record it as we had no video then. Ann rang everyone she could think of to let them know and settled down to watch it with my daugher Sarah. After the interview we met Harry Gration, David Oxley, Emlyn Hughes and the editor of the *Sunday Times*, who, although from Bradford, hadn't seen a live Rugby League match for years!

Only the result spoilt an otherwise perfect day - if only Schofield and Crooks had kicked the goals, if only Steve Evans had got away on the halfway line in the last seconds. If only!

☐ We beat Leeds 8 - 4 in the 1947 Challenge Cup Final. Bert Cook kicked two goals for Leeds, Emilyn Walters and myself scored tries for Bradford and Ernest Ward dropped a goal. Willie Davies won the Lance Todd Trophy.

A most remarkable event took place in our Wembley dressing room. Ernest had received the Cup from the Duke of Gloucester and, after walking on air, planted the Cup on the dressing room table. Our manager, Dai Rees, said, "Boys, you have never mentioned money since we have been here in London. I pay tribute to that." Money was secondary, we went to Wembley to win, with pride in our team, wearing our famous red, amber and black jerseys, and for the City of Bradford. Can you imagine such an approach in sport today?

What a magnificent reception we received returning from Wembley on the following Monday night in Town Hall Square, by the Lord Mayor. The roads to the city centre were packed, every inch of space outside the City Hall was taken up. I hope and pray that I will live to see another such historical happening in our great city of Bradford.

☐ If I had to list the top half dozen major developments involving the promotion of Rugby League, *Open Rugby* magazine would certainly be amongst them. Down the years it has been a massive boom to the game. It has been a far better publicist for the game than the game's own publicity department. However, it was *Open Rugby* which sent me on the worst journey of my life.

It seemed a good idea at the time. In association with PL Travel, *Open Rugby* arranged a train - "Open Rugby League

Express", to the first test match of the 1990 Ashes Series at Wembley (the Odsal of the South). It was only £19.50 and it was supposed to leave Halifax at 7.00 am. That was its starting point and it would then go to Bradford, Leeds, Wakefield, Doncaster, Sheffield, Wembley Central and London Euston, the latter presumably for wives and girlfriends who preferred shopping to watching rugby. On the travel notes, which I still have, it told us to "arrive in good time and check the platform of departure carefully".

So my brother Charlie and I duly turned up in very good time along with dozens of others. Remember, this was very late October; it was pitch black at that time of the morning and it was freezing cold. What's more, Halifax Station five years ago had absolute zilch facilities. At about 7.30 am there was no sign of the "Open Rugby League Express" and hypothermia was setting in. Then a policeman appeared and announced that the train would be an hour and a half late!

By now the regular scheduled trains had started to come and go, but we were all hanging on for our special. A Bradford train pulled in and a rather fetching young lady picked up her travelling bag and boarded. As she lifted the bag, a skirt slowly slid off it on to the floor; she never noticed. Being a gentleman, I picked up the skirt and pursued her onto the train and restored it to her. The train must have been late, for as I tried to get off, the doors closed and refused to open and I was carted off to Bradford, to the obvious amusement of everybody on the platform, some of whom were in stitches. After the initial blind panic subsided, I realised that at least I was in the warmth and could pick up the special when it came through Bradford. At Bradford the cafe was open, so I went for a cup of tea along with maybe a hundred or so other folk bound for Wembley.

Just as I finished the tea, there was an announcement telling all the rugby fans to get on the incoming train to Leeds. When we got to Leeds there was another announcement telling us all to make our own way to London on the scheduled trains. It was one of my worst nightmares come true. Normally in London I just freaked out and blindly followed Charlie who seemed to understand the tube and all that crazy rushing around stuff. At least he always managed to get us to Wembley at Cup Final time.

The train from Leeds was heaving with all the extra hundreds of rugby fans and, just to complicate matters, it was going to Kings Cross rather than Euston. It was in fact the 9.18. The "Open Rugby" train had been scheduled to leave Leeds at 8.02. Amazingly the scheduled train got to Kings Cross at 12.05, which was just about the time the 'special' should have been arriving at Wembley Central. God knows what was happening to the folk back at Halifax!

At Kings Cross I was mystified as to what to do, but at least there was no need to face the dreaded ticket machines as our tickets were valid to take us to Wembley. I would probably still be there if I'd had to get another ticket. To my horror, I found myself accosted by a young couple from Leeds who were in the same predicament, but they had never ever been to London in their lives. They were more terrified than me! What's more they expected me to get them to Wembley and for some reason the girl thought that telling me her mother was responsible for the catering on the "Open Rugby" train would somehow comfort me.

I got them there. We were dead lucky. The trains were not running once we got a couple of stations up the tube line and buses were laid on to take passengers to their destinations. That suited me and my two disciples down to the ground, as one of them was going to Wembley. You could actually see where you were going.

Ten minutes into the match our Charlie scrambled breathlessly into his seat next to me; he had run from Wembley Central, having waited at Leeds for the "Open Rugby". He had paid for it and he was going on it!

It was a good job Britain won a wonderful victory, 19-12. At least everyone was happy when they caught the train back from Wembley Central. It was more or less on time, although it was the oldest, grottiest rolling stock known to British Rail. On the way back, some lads were having a good laugh, reliving the incident with the prat who got carted off the Bradford that morning. You should have seen their faces drop when I told them how early I had got to the game! Everything was hunky-dory until we got to Leeds. We were on time - it was about 10.20. An hour later we were still sitting there and it became apparent that the train was going nowhere. Nobody bothered to tell us that the guards in Manchester had gone on strike. When we did find out there was a mad rush to get the last scheduled train to Bradford and Halifax. We arrived in Halifax after midnight: I had begun to wonder if I would ever see the place again. After that it was easy-peasy; just a six mile walk to Ripponden. I could cope with that!

What really upset me in all this was the fact that *Open Rugby* never apologised for the 'Express from Hell'. I have every issue of *Open Rugby* but I'll never go on one of their 'specials' again. That's for sure.

☐ My most memorable day in Rugby League was refereeing the curtain-raiser to the Leeds versus Wigan Challenge Cup Final. We were making such an honour a family weekend away, but my daughter was not too keen; she had never shown any interest in the great game. It was a case of, "Your dad's refereeing, you're going," followed by much face-pulling.

However, come the day, she was captivated and then captured by the whole occasion and came home requesting a season ticket for the following season. Mind you I have a feeling it was Francis Cummins, as much as Rugby League itself, that captured her!

☐ Just before Fev went to Wembley in 1983, we bought a video recorder. Brilliant, I thought, my mother is coming round to look after the kids while we go to the 'Twin Towers', so she can tape the match for us.

"Everything is set, all you have to do is press record. OK?" We set off for the train.

Now my mum isn't too good with anything mechanical and when we returned very late the same evening, totally drunk on the atmosphere of one of the best days ever, and just a little bit smug thinking we could re-live the day, we put on the video.

"Oh, you've re-wound it then," says I.

"No I just pressed record like you said."

"But this tape hasn't moved, it's still got Bagpuss and bloody Postman Pat on it."

She had done everything right except turn it on. We'd missed everything that had been on the telly about Fev and the match and all the interviews.

Fortunately we copied someone else's tape and when we sat down to watch it, the very first words spoken on it were by John Hill, the guy who does the match videos now, and he said, "I think Featherstone Rovers will shock the Rugby League world on Saturday." How the hell did he know that? Anyway that tape is very precious and I keep it well away from my mum.

☐ On the morning of the Final, I arrived at 7.30 am to my coach departure point, in order to supervise my fifty-two young schoolboys on their journey into the history books, only to find that our 'luxury coach' had been replaced by a museum charabanc. One of the town's most celebrated drivers lay underneath the vehicle, size ten boots protruding, polished segs and all. Choice language drifted to my hearing with an accompaniment of dull hammering. I broke into a cold sweat.

The celebrated gentleman driver, known locally for his lack of tolerance, stared at me coldly, challenging me not to speak and spitting out a phlegmy mixture of catarrh, flaky dust and oil, exclaiming, "It's nowt! Bolt's nobbut sheared off t'prop shaft! It'll get us there ..."

I allowed a hearty exhalation of breath, only to be cut short prematurely by, "... at thirty miles an hour!!"

The 'Twin Towers' misted before my eyes and I sought consolation and optimism, some earlier good luck omen or sign, from the cup run, that would comfort and reassure me. I found it in the form of the game at Batley. My friend had been allocated a full row of directors' seats to himself, such was his passion and enthusiasm for the game. The rest of the committee sat on the row behind to give him room to vent his feelings at the opposition and the ref, and not to be directly associated with him. As the game progressed, so did my friend, shuffling along the line of seats towards the players' tunnel, in verbal reach of the ref when he departed the field at half time. It had worked! My friend had shuffled along for eighty minutes and we had won our way to Wembley and now it was our turn to shuffle.

Getting there, well that's another tale! On time? Just! Mind you, I was last out of our paddock in the ground, drinking it all in, shuffled back to the coach and was last on, but we'd won!

☐ You only ever hear *Abide With Me* at Cup Finals and funerals. Probably your happiest and saddest moments in life. Maybe you join in at Wembley without really examining the beauty and pathos of the words. Only the first two verses are usually printed in Cup Final programmes. Perhaps you've never seen the last three verses, particularly the final two:

Swift to its close ebbs out life's little day,
Earth's joys grow dim, its glories pass away.
Change and decay in all around I see,
O thou, who changest not, abide with me.

I fear no foe, with thee at hand to bless,
Ills have no weight and tears no bitterness.
Where is death's sting? Where, grave, they victory?
I triumph still, if thou abide with me.

The exquisite sadness of those lines made me wonder many times about the writer's situation and state of mind. Who, when and what was he? How could I find out? I mused out loud one day.

"No problem," I was told. "I'll get you my FA Cup Final, Liverpool versus Sunderland programme from 1992."

"The scene is set in the fishing village of Brixham, Devon, in 1847, where Henry Francis Lythe, a charitable and popular Vicar at All Saints Church, was advised, due to his failing health, that he would have to leave the work and the people he cared so much about and travel abroad to the warmer climate of the Mediterranean where he could rest. The last Sunday before his departure from England, although quite weak, he addressed his congregation as normal, but knowing in his heart that it was probably for the last time. This was such a physically and emotionally tiring experience for him that it had left him weaker than normal.

On returning to Berry Head House, the family home, Lyte's family thought he had gone for a rest, but on his return one hour later, he gave a family member a piece of paper on which he had written 'Abide With Me', accompanied with a few notes indicating a tune to this hymn.

He left England later that year and arrived in Nice, never to return to his home town."

So one of England's most popular hymns was written and composed in less time than it takes to complete a football match!

Reverend Lyte pre-dated any form of rugby as we know it, but I hope he is happy for his great hymn to be associated with The Greatest Game.

Keighley Were On A Roll
Memorable Games

☐ It was one of the greatest games of all time - fantastic rugby, breathtaking tries. I'm talking about the 1985 Challenge Cup Final between

Hull and Wigan. There were 99,801 folk at Wembley for it. Steve Donlan, a modest and unassuming chap, played at centre for Wigan that day and he was interviewed about the game at his home a little later. This is how the interview went:

"A wonderful game, wasn't it, Steve?"

"Yes."

"What do you remember about the game?"

"Nothing in particular."

"What did you do after the game?"

"Just went to the tea rooms, had a cuppa tea and a piece of cake. Battenberg it was, really nice. Never had any before. I had David Stephenson's piece too."

☐ Eddie Waring introduced me to the game with the BBC2 Floodlit Trophy in the mid-1960s, but living in London there was no chance of seeing a live match.

During an early-in-the-year-visit to Mum and Dad at Skipton, the local paper revealed that Keighley were playing Wigan in Round Three of the Challenge Cup, an all ticket game, I think. However, Dad and me managed to get in, despite arriving late, but because of the huge crowd it was almost half time before we found a place where we could see the pitch.

Shortly after the second half started we were distracted by raised voices a few feet away.

"Eh up, tha's in my place!"

"Well, why did you leave it then."

"I went for some tea."

"Ah, well, now, you've had your tea and I've got your place. Tha should've brought a flask!"

"I shall thump thee."

"Aye, alright, but do it after t'match, there's a good game on 'ere."

Shortly after, we were all urged to 'budge up a bit' and the late arrival was able to squeeze in amongst us and the pair were last seen sharing a bag of toffees and cheering on their respective teams.

As to the actual game, the record books reveal that Wigan won 11-2. Sadly I have no recollection of events that took place on the pitch, but the thing that really upsets me is the fact that I saw the great Billy Boston play, and score, in my first live Rugby League game - and I can't remember it.

☐ I guess we've been spoiled by the multiple replays of TV coverage and the chance to relive the game via video. This explains why I tend to remember incidents, not actual games, and two of the most vivid happened in ordinary, run-of-the-mill matches, not in any of the Wembley finals, test matches, cup ties or even grand finals I've been lucky enough to attend over the past thirty-odd years.

The first incident happened around February 1970, when Sunday games were as infrequent as tries in a Union game. Keighley played Hunslet in a re-arranged league game. No 'Cougars' or 'Hawks' back then, just two teams playing out the season, though in those days Keighley started playing out the season about August!

The pitch had a covering of three to four inches of snow and all the lines were marked in a vivid blue and, to complete the mystique, an orange ball was used. Keighley won 26-8 with right-winger, Ken Roberts, sliding in for four tries. I still wonder what hallucinogenic was in that half time pie! To add to his misery, we pelted the Parksiders' No. 5 with snowballs everytime he came near where we stood. A truly brilliant day for a league-mad eleven year old.

The second incident also happened at Lawkholme about twelve months later when, thanks to an easier fixture list, Keighley were on a roll with eight consecutive wins, going in to play Widnes, who were just building the team that was to take them to Wembley. In a close, tense game, Keighley took the lead with four penalty goals to two, but Widnes came back and scored a try in the bottom left hand corner to get within a point. Their full-back, Ray Dutton, lined up the kick on the touchline. As the crowd jeered, he went through his methodical routine: tee-up, look at the posts, four steps back, look at the post again, couple of deep breaths, left foot forward. Then a hand reached out of the low paddock on the stand side and pulled his right leg from under him; down he went.

Pandemonium broke out, referee, touch judges, players, officials, police all converged and started arguing the toss. The crowd were in hysterics. Eventually, order was restored. Dutton re-took the kick which sailed hopelessly wide, as did a later easy penalty attempt, his confidence shot! Keighley won 8-7; a real Rugby League score, not one of the basket ball scores of today.

The story even made the front page of the *Bradford T & A* with a picture of the culprit remonstrating with a couple of bobbies and the ref. Keighley of course were severely repremanded by the Rugby League, ie told to go stand in the bottom corner of the League table the following season. As to the miscreant himself, no life ban or warning as to future conduct, but the rumour around town was that the Board paid him a win bonus!

☐ Many years before BARLA thought to organise Rugby League for junior players, enterprising northern kids just got on with it themselves. I lived in Ackworth but went to school in Pontefract and one of my classmates, Tony Gallon, arranged to bring a team of fourteen and fifteen year olds over from Pontefract to play a scratch team of Ackworth youths.

The match was arranged for a balmy May evening, the venue was the cabbage patch at the bottom of Dicky Sykes Lane and the Pontefract team, led by the redoubtable Vic Greendale, duly arrived on the ten past seven South Yorkshire bus. Both teams walked from the bus stop down Dicky Sykes Lane, nervously weighing each other up.

"There's more o' them than us," one of my team mates pointed out and he was quite right. As co-organiser of the event I could not let this pass and, after much haggling, Pontefract lent us three players and the game kicked off with seventeen-a-side.

The match was of course played under League rules, unlimited tackles in those far-off days, but certain local practices had to be obeyed. Anyone kicking to touch and landing the ball in Harry Townend's garden, or hitting the wall of Ada Pritchard's terrace, had to face the wrath of their respective owners and if the ball (the only one we had) was confiscated, then the match was immediately forfeit to the other team. There had been some discussion beforehand as to whether we should enlighten the Pontefract team to these possible local difficulties, but Jimmy Seal, the owner of the ball, had insisted.

Harry Townend, as well as being possessed of an uncertain temper, had one other claim to fame. A powerfully built man, the Nostell pit blacksmith could sit on the wooden settle at the back of his living room and spit over an open pan of taties bubbling away on his blazing fire, without ever hitting the pan. You try it from twelve feet, it is not as easy as it sounds.

The match got underway, refereed by one player from each team, and after the first few punch-ups we all settled down to enjoy the game. It quickly became apparent that we were fairly evenly matched apart from the Pontefract skipper, Vic Greendale, who was a class above the rest of us. By half time Pontefract were twenty points in front and it looked like nothing could stop them. We were further disadvantaged when Keith Woodhouse, our classy centre, sloped off just before the interval, as he had a heavy date with a local sporting lady. His absence however, led to our revival.

Running diagonally across the pitch was a well worn footpath which led from Dicky Sykes Lane up to Hemsworth pit fields and several men had already walked through the middle of our game on their way to night shift at Hemsworth. Just after half time, a local youth, Arthur Carlisle, was making his way down the path when he paused to enquire the score. On being told that we were trailing by twenty points

and a man short, Arthur said, "Rayt, I'll laike for ten minutes."

Now Arthur was nineteen, four or five years older than the rest of us, and in the few minutes he played his extra size and confidence totally unnerved our opponents. Despite the handicap of pit boots and snap tin smacking against his backside, he scored four tries, converted them all himself and flattened Vic Greendale with the kind of tackle Les Boyd would have been proud of. At that point the scores were level and the Pontefract team immediately went on sit down strike in the middle of the pitch, complaining that Arthur was too old.

"I'll have to be off anyway," said our hero and, pausing only to pick up his jacket, he strode off to the pit. We were soon up to strength again, however. Arthur's sister, Nora, had been an interested spectator, but on her brother's departure, she offered to fill his place. Even though she was a couple of years older than us, the Pontefract team did not object to a mere girl playing. Little did they know! Nora was destined to become a physical education teacher and a county hockey player, and she certainly educated the Pontefract mob. Within a couple of minutes of joining the game, she had felled their flying winger into a patch of stinging nettles and launched a violent, physical and verbal assault on Vic Greendale.

The match was over as a contest and we ran out easy winners. All in all not the kind of match that made local, let alone national, headlines, but one to remember all the same.

☐ I have a vivid memory of Hull's centre, Roy Francis, running the length of the field for an interception try which was disallowed. I was really upset for him - it's funny how you take such things so seriously as a young child.

The Boulevard's reputation for crowd involvement is nothing new. My dad told me that as a young policeman in the 1930s, he was first assigned to Boulevard duties. Before the start he was pulled aside by the inspector and told, "There are a lot of men using very bad language in that stand. I want you to go over there and if necessary evict them!"

So Dad nervously paced in front of the Threepenny Stand, occasionally glaring at the worst offenders, when it gradually dawned on him that he was being set up - simply everyone in the stand was using bad language.

In another pre-war game, Hull had a couple of players sent off in a match against Salford. The mood of the Threepenny Stand grew ever uglier and when the final whistle went, hundreds poured over the railings and headed for the referee. The few police on duty, including my dad, had a head start in the chase to catch the unfortunate official, when a great clod of earth launched in the general direction of the referee fell just short of its target and knocked my dad's helmet clean off his head.

☐ It's hard to prove that any game has ever been fixed, but there are a lot of Saints fans who know better. We played Wigan one Good Friday and it was at the time when they were going to introduce two divisions. Wigan were on the border-line and it was a toss-up whether they or York would end up in Division Two. I'm not kidding, Wigan were really dire at that time.

It was obvious that the Saints were going to let Wigan win, probably to make sure they retained their best gate of the season for next year. Two of Saints' players knocked on about fourteen times in Wigan's twenty-five and, although Saints had about ninety percent of the match, Wigan scored on both their attacks and won about 12-2. At one point, Saints' hooker burst clear about forty yards out, he had an absolutely clear run to the posts. Wigan weren't interested in even chasing him. He must have realised that he was going to score, so he slowed down and headed for a corner instead and managed to get himself tackled by running sixty-five yards instead of forty.

On Easter Monday, we played Widnes at Knowsley Road and Basil Lowe, the Saints' secretary, announced over the loudspeaker that York had only drawn with Leeds and so Wigan would get a place in the First Division. Well, I remember the crowd booed him off the tannoy and booed Saints off the field.

Any Saints fan who was there will swear it's true. In fact I know some people who have never been back to Saints since.

☐ One of the big regrets of my Rugby League spectating is never to have seen the great Salford team of the 1930s. Well, actually I did see them, but then again I didn't see them, if you see what I mean. In 1938 I was a schoolboy in Wigan and mad keen on Rugby League. I had a cousin who was four years older than me and he was a big fan too. He would take me to games with him. This was alright generally, but not at Christmas. Our family was a small one and, as families do at Christmas, there tends to be a get-together. Every Christmas my mother took me to my gran's and my cousin went too. Unfortunately for me, my mother didn't hold with me going to Central Park to watch rugby on Christmas Day. Normally she encouraged me to follow the game, but Christmas Day was an exception. It really rankled with me that I wasn't allowed to go, but my cousin always could.

In 1938, Christmas Day fell on Sunday and so there were no games to worry about. Instead

Wigan were to play the great Gus Risman's Salford on the Monday - Boxing Day, so I could go. Would you believe it? The fog came down and, although I knew Wigan and Salford were out there, I could see virtually nothing. Occasionally a ghostly figure would flit passed us down the touchline, but that would have been the touch judge. I remember the Salford winger, big Barney Hudson, coming to the touchline near us and shouting up at the press box that he had scored a try. What a farce! God knows why they played the game.

I never did get to see Salford properly. The War came and Salford shut up shop until 1945, by which time their great team had broken up.

Would You Knock Your Own Son Out?
Playing Memories

☐ I never felt like I was a hard man. Don't get me wrong, I wouldn't take any shit, I never backed off, but it's the press that give you titles and I'll tell you what, some of these so-called hard men start to fret a bit when it comes to the three W's away. Wigan, Warrington and Workington. I've known a few so-called tough guys get Workingtonitis.

There's none of 'em could have held a candle to Willis Fawley. Now he was a hard man. We

once played in a game at Halifax. We both went to tackle the same man. He must have ducked as I went in and I caught Willis straight in the gob. His front teeth sailed out as sweet as a nut. As we got up I picked the two teeth up and put them beside the post. When I came back up into the line, I said to Willis, "I've put thi teeth down again' that post."

He said, "Huh!"

I repeated what I'd said. He just grunted. He didn't even know he'd had them knocked out. He was as hard as the main road, was Willis.

I learned a lot off him, but I mainly learned from the way the Lancashire forwards play. We only played four games a year against them then. I looked forward to Lancashire games so I could study their forwards. I liked the way they let the ball go to the support. I looked forward to all my games, it never bothered me who we played, I used to think I was as good as anybody. I loved it. When we were coming off the field at the end of the game, all I could think about was, "Who are we playing next week?"

☐ There are downsides to women's rugby. We had a great new player, she only lasted two weeks and then she got pregnant. We can be more temperamental; if it's the time of the month, or we've had a tiff with boyfriends, it affects our play more than men's ... men are

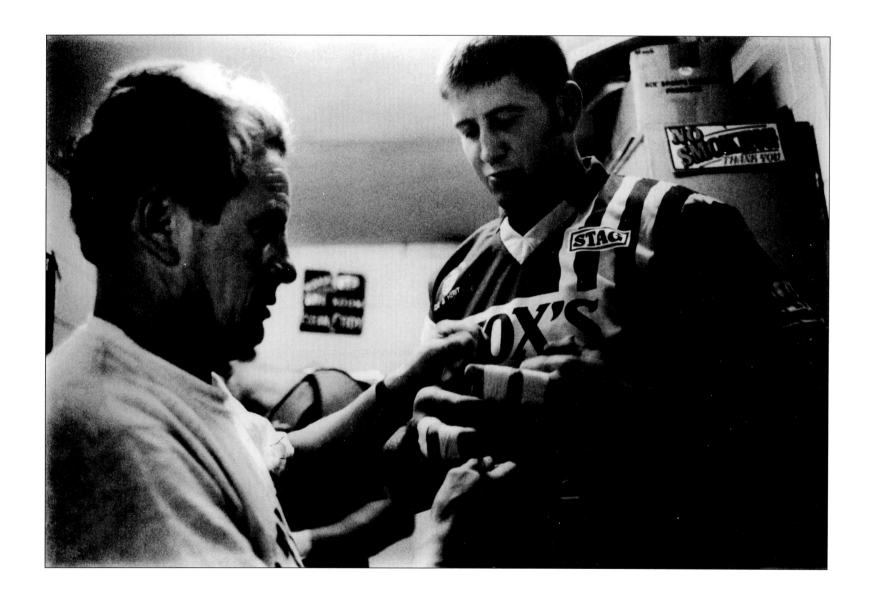

more heartless. The same with praising the other team. You never see men applauding their opponents if they do a ninety yard try, we do. We'll be pissed off, but you can admire it. We don't criticise too much. If we think, "You stupid get," for giving a bad pass, we don't say it, because a woman might walk off the pitch.

☐ We were playing New Zealand Select Thirteen: a friendly in 1958. Two of the New Zealanders had been carried off on stretchers. When it came to the second half I turned to Vince Karalius and said "Have you seen how many they've got on?" Vince counted them up and realised they had a full thirteen. I told him that Tom Mitchell had said they could use replacements for injured players. Vinty went storming over to Mr Mitchell and said "Eh Tom, what's the use of me keep banging 'em and getting 'em barrowed off if you keep sending some other buggers back on?"

☐ I've only felt sorry for somebody on a field once. I was playing for the Robins against Barrow. Somehow I'd been left wide and I was half going for the man with the ball and half going for the next bloke. He skipped past me. I got that upset I chased him and when I caught him I banged him. He was out cold when they took him off. After the game I saw him in the club house, I kept looking across to him and he was still not all there. I felt a bit sorry.

There were ways to test blokes out. The more you got stuck into Colin Dixon, the better he played. But somebody like Don Vines might back down. He once bit me and when I rolled on top of him to give him one, he said, "It wasn't me!"

☐ I was a late starter in the game. I hardly played anything at school. The gym teacher hated me. One day he left us in the gym and when he came back he caned every single lad for acting about. I had a pair of right thin shorts on and I had weals on my arse for days after. We were having our tea on the Sunday and my cousin mentioned it. My dad took my trousers down and had a look. On the Monday my dad went up to the school and had the teacher by the throat. The master made my life a misery after that, so I could never enjoy my sport.

The first game I actually saw was when Blackpool Borough came into the league. Old Ernest Ward played centre and Denzil Webster, both top of their class. They stuck in my mind, that and the fact that it was the first time I'd been anywhere on my own. I don't think my dad ever saw a game of Rugby League. When I started playing, all my mother worried about was that I'd get too big-headed. I remember her saying, "I've been talking to so and so and she said, 'He's getting a right funny bugger is your Terry, he doesn't talk to anybody.'" Because everybody gets to know you, they think you ought to know them.

☐ Batley were playing Wigan at Central Park; both teams needed the points. The Wigan front row were: Egan, Gee and Banks. Batley had a set move when near an opponent's line; it involved both second row forwards. With me in the second row at that time was a seventeen stone man named John Brown, from the Salford area. We were only yards from the Wigan line. Joe Golby took up his position as acting half-back behind the man playing the ball. John took up his position on one side of Joe and I took up my position on the other side. I had to make a lot of racket shouting to Joe to get the ball and rushing forward when Joe picked up the ball. John, not making any noise, moved forward. Joe put a perfect pass straight into John's hefty arms, who crashed over to score. My job as decoy was done and I ambled over the line to congratulate my team mate.

Waiting on the line was the irritated Mr Banks; he had no time to tackle me, but stuck out a ham-like fist and bonked me on the nose. I sat on the turf in a daze, with claret streaming down my nose. John came over all smiles,

"We've done it again, mate," he chortled.

"I've a better idea for next time," I replied. "Next time I will do the scoring and you can do the running."

Mr Banks stood on the try line smiling.

☐ I remember the build-up in 1961, Dave Bolton was always leaking, always one for the toilet. Eric Ashton would tape himself up repeatedly, as would Billy Boston. In 1961 they stuck a needle in Boston's knee - I'm not kidding; I wouldn't have done to a horse what they did to Billy for killing the pain of that knee injury he had. Billy always used to have a shoulder strap, where the buckle was they used to put padding soaked in ether, so he could breathe a bit easier. He had a bad injury at Leeds when his breastbone got caved in.

In 1961 we should have murdered 'em. That bloody try at the end, they were jammy! Sayer's behind the play, the ball just to the left of the posts ... he gives it to Brian and I'm coming through like an express train. I says, "Give it here, Brian," then bump ... the ball shoots out. Huddart picks up, gives it Large, who gives it Vollenhoven and that's it. Mind you, Griffiths should have been tighter on Vollenhoven, but it was too late. A spur of the moment thing, but it turned the game. We knew where the dangers were; that back three, they worked as a team, the

rest were individuals. The back three were the real work horses of the team, always involved in the game.

Mind you, what memories of Wembley. What about 1958 when Cherrington tackled Southward. I never saw Southward - he was about to put the ball down, but Norman did and he caught him. I don't know what it is about playing at Wembley, but it seems to go very quickly.

I recall lining up with my team mates before one final and we were being presented to General Montgomery, the special guest. As he came towards me, I says to Eric Ashton, "You shouldn't need to tell him who I am."

Monty looked at me and said, "Why? Who are you?"

"I fought for you at El Alamein, Sir."

"Did you?" Mind you, he must have been bloody daft to believe that!

"What regiment?"

"Girl Guides."

He patted me on the shoulder and said, "The finest regiment ever."

Then after the match as we were going up to the reception, Bill Fallowfield comes up to me and says that when they were going up to the Royal Box, Monty turned to him and asked, "What regiment did that lad say he was in?" He said that he was cringing with embarrassment.

☐ I was a winger in the 1930s. Side-stepping and coming through on the burst were what the game was about. Today they don't seem to read the game - there's no class anymore.

Our pay in those days was £4 a win, £3 a draw, £2 a loss and half a crown tea money. A lot of players were builders or dockers and trained after work.

Jack Davies was my mentor, he taught me a lot of tricks on the punch ball and could run one hundred yards in eleven seconds with the ball in his hands - fourteen stone, all muscle.

I always used to go onto the pitch with a side parting - well greased, lots of Brylcream on - and I was noted for interception tries. At the time Castleford had a scrum half, a New Zealander, who had a habit of coming on the wing and hitting the winger to put him off. I managed to intercept and, chased by Castleford's Captain - Atkinson - I ran forty-five yards to score. As I stood up, Atkinson came quickly towards me. I expected a punch, but instead he shook my hand and said, "John, that's the grandest try I've seen at Castleford." I left the pitch with my hair the same as when I went on and shocked by the praise given to me by an opposing player.

☐ I once visited an old player from the 1930s. He was a devout Catholic; you could tell from all the religious pictures and figurines about the house. Anyway, at one point his wife went out of the room and he told me that one Wednesday his team went to play in London against Streatham and Mitcham. They went down on an early train and the chairman told the players they were going to a brothel that he apparently used when he was down in the capital. However, our devout Catholic excused himself and went straight to the ground, complete with all the valuables entrusted to him by the naughty players and directors. His side lost the game and the newspaper reported their display as 'lethargic'.

Curiosity got the better of the innocent player and he asked what the brothel had been like. Nobody answered his question, but one player, obviously a bit put out, told him it hadn't been worth it. It had cost him six bob and he had only got five bob losing pay.

☐ One season Alex Murphy was in charge of Leigh's first team. It was in Alex's contract that he had to attend home 'A' team matches. Alex hardly ever went. He did go one time though when they played Blackpool Borough 'A', who were absolute rubbing rags. He never watched the game, however. We were winning 24-0 just before the half time whistle, when Blackpool scored a try to make it 24-4. The 'A' team coach

was furious that they had let in the try. At that point Alex appeared and asked what the score was; 24-4 he was told. He blew his top and yelled, "How can we be losing 24-4 to this lot? I'll bloody give the half time talk." The poor 'A' team coach never had the chance to explain they were winning. In the dressing room Alex went into over-drive. Paint was coming off the walls. He finally asked if anyone had anything to say and one of the props said, "But we're winning Alex." Quick as a flash, Alex said, "I know. Imagine what I'd be like if you were losing."

☐ When they had a Leigh Hall of Fame night, Eddie Hemmings interviewed some of the players. When he interviewed Joe Walsh, one of Leigh's greatest wingers, he asked why Leigh had such a great team spirit when he played? Joe replied, "We drank a lot of beer".

☐ I made my debut against Bramley. I put my coat on a peg and somebody growled at me, "That's mine young 'un." I had to move my coat three times before I found one that nobody else wanted. They talk about team spirit in the old days, you'd all on making friends with your own team! There were some good men though. Harry Street went to see the selectors and offered to switch positions so I could get in. He never told me and I didn't find out until a long time after.

I'd gone down for a trial after 'Pip' Churchill, who worked as an apprentice at Pollards Bearings with me, told me that they were starting an Under 16½ team. I came sticking my chest out as a centre, I was rubbish. They tried me at full back and on the wing. We played at Hunslet and Ken Hirst ran rings round me. Eventually I settled at loose forward and then went to second-row. By the time I got to Bradford I was at blind-side prop and at Hull KR, after Artie Beetson got a knock, I played open side.

☐ There was a testimonial game at Widnes. The Chemics were playing Liverpool Football Club at soccer for someone or other. The Liverpool players couldn't believe the size of some of the Widnes lads, but were more taken aback by the spartan conditions in the Widnes dressing rooms. I suppose they were used to better things at Anfield. After the game one of the Liverpool players stuck his head round the Widnes dressing room door and said, "Excuse me lads, where do I plug in me hair dryer?" Glyn Shaw just glared at him and he disappeared sharp.

☐ Moving round clubs was frowned on. Everybody used to say, "He's a good clubman," meaning that they expected you to stay with one club. In 1967 I got an offer from Eastern Suburbs, they wanted me to take my wife and family over for a fortnight to see how I liked it. Bradford wouldn't let me go. I might not have liked it anyhow. I hate Aussies, on the whole they're arrogant and they don't shake hands properly at the end of a match when they're beat. I had a lot of time for Artie Beetson, but he was my team mate for a while. On the field in internationals we went at one another as though we'd never met.

I don't like the Aussie style of play either. Everything's changed to suit them, they never had a hooker worth two bob, so they did away with them. In the 1960s Jack Gibson, the coach at Eastern Suburbs, started going to America and bringing ideas back for coaching and training. Then it got and got while they were playing to statistics.

☐ Harry Woods played for Wigan Highfield, who became London Highfield for one season in the 1930s. He told me his routine for match days in London. He was a foundry worker, was Harry. London played their home games on Wednesday nights, so he had to catch a train down to London at 2.00 pm which got in about 6.00 pm. Then he travelled to the White City to play the game. He would catch the midnight train back to Lancashire and hope it arrived on time at 4.00 am, so he could get to work on time at 5.00 am. I remember him telling me that Highfield once beat Wigan in London. Wigan tried to blame it on the floodlights, but Harry wouldn't have that. They just got beat fair and square.

☐ My last test match was in 1932 at Belle Vue. They came to me and said, "You're playing against a very good wing threequarter today - he's only a young lad, but he's brilliant. We want you to get him off the field as soon as you can ... the stretcher cannot come on soon enough!" I looked at them and said that during the whole of my test match career I had never done that and I had no intention of starting now. "Well, we want you to do it today!" I was adamant of course and told them that if I had to kill someone to win a game of football, I would retire straightaway.

I remember playing against the St Helens Recs and a seventeen year old lad called Albert Pimblett. He was a schoolboy prodigy - brilliant! I was a Wigan player by this time in the mid 1930s and I'm marking him. He looks at me and I can see he's frightened, so I tell him that there is nothing to be worried about. Anyhow, he gets a ball on the blind side and I just pick him up and put his feet over the touch line. "Why didn't you bloody well kill him," yelled our full-back, Jim Sullivan. I asked him if he would knock his own son out, after all he was just a boy. Some of the Recs' committeemen came to me afterwards and thanked me for the way I had treated this young lad. After all, isn't this the way the game should be played?

"Now some of you say, it is the north wind who has woven the clothes we wear. And I say, aye it was the north wind."
The Prophet
Kahlil Gibran

BRAVE NEW WORLD

Northern Have Become The Bulls
The Super League Future

☐ Geez, I'm getting old. Cynical about the present, sentimental about the past. Lacking vision and ambition. I'm no good with change. Plodding sloth, fixed habits are more my line. Hence all the changes in Rugby League right now leave me cold. Super League doesn't sound so super, Northern have become the Bulls. Maybe not so bad in themselves, but then again, maybe symptomatic of a radical, scary future.

And on top of all that, now they're going to develop Odsal. What is the world coming to? "Sportsworld", "Musicworld", 250-bedroom hotels, not to mention "... interested parties from the Middle East, USA and Europe ..." Odsal with a roof? For heaven's sake!

I must admit to taking some comfort from the fact that most of it has been said before, but nothing ever changes. The "Wally Lewis is coming ..." feeling about even these most serious of plans offers me some hope. Let's be honest, for as long as there's been an Odsal, there's been a plan in the pipeline to make it

"Wembley of the North", "envy of the world", or whatever. Pipelines and pipe dreams seem to overlap in the world of development.

Odsal means a lot to me. Maybe even more since I'm miles away. A bit like exiled Irishmen, sentimentality grows in direct proportion to

> **"The Director and his students stood for a short time watching a game of centrifugal Bumble-puppy ... It's madness. Nowadays the controllers won't approve of any new game unless it can be shown that it requires at least as much apparatus as the most complicated of existing games."**
>
> **Brave New World**
> **Aldous Huxley**

distance. Anyway my dreams of Odsal have nothing to do with sliding roofs or hotels. Mine is a dream of childhood, of growing up and the seasons turning, of history, of life itself. All the memories, the feelings. As a kid, Odsal was the light on my hill. All roads led to Odsal. Part of me says they still do.

Where else is the clash and majesty of the elements so strong? Okay, so 'majesty' is a word

only an idiot living ten thousand miles away might use, but humour me a while, this is sentiment stretched to its rosy best. And what's wrong with that?

From shirt-sleeved August, through flag-whipped autumn and Siberian winter. Flushed faces to chafed hands and stamping feet. Wintergreen, warm pies, tobacco and damp coats.

It's a place of heroes and giants. I remember once as a boy standing in the centre of the pitch at a deserted Odsal. The atmosphere was physical. I felt ten feet tall, but dwarfed by the place. Mystical stuff. Just think of the greats. The gods of mythology who have stridden the place, Ward, Bevan, Boston ... The big games. Tests. Finals. The place was ever much more than railway sleepers, muck and weeds. Don't try telling me there wasn't magic in the air.

Mind you, most of that place went with the Old Stand. Now, I suppose it's neither developed, nor is it left alone. A bit like "Save the Tiger" and stick him in a concrete and steel cage. If that's saving, God help the tiger.

But whatever happens will happen. Not much I can do. The price of progress is a high one. But

I hope they retain at least the name. Odsal. It's synonymous with Bradford, with Rugby League, with sport. It would be nice if sometimes the powers that be could be humble enough to show respect for their past. Progress and change don't have to mean the same.

Calling Odsal something along the lines of Bradford Superdome would be historical vandalism on a par to asking Rolf Harris to touch up the Sistine Chapel, as inspired as if the original founders had called Bradford 'Area of Hilly Land with Houses'.

So I'm out of touch. Living in the past. Even the memories of Cas running riot and rain dripping down the back of your neck heal with time. And distance. It's not everybody's cup of tea, isn't Odsal. But I love it and I don't think I'm the only one. Just a word to the developers: leave us something. Something on which we can rest our memories. Leave us the name, eh fellas.

☐ It was a normal Saturday. I had done the shopping and was settling down to an afternoon listening to the radio while doing the housework. Suddenly the world was different. An important announcement from Wigan. Who had we signed? Who had we sacked? I found myself standing, staring open-mouthed at the stereo. I was stunned that the seemingly self-interested chairman of the entire RFL had managed to take on board a decision of such magnitude. Unanimously at that! I can remember thinking that at last Rugby League, the best game in the world, had got the kick-up the backside it needed and was going to become a national game. A national summer game at that!

Rugby League was to be brought to the attention of those people who adore the antics of gaily dressed harlequins who pat a round ball about a field. Harlequins whose wages far outstrip their talent and courage and whose nefarious activities accompany my breakfast every day.

Seven days later, things were back to normal. Rugby League was still an exclusively northern sport, but with a very expensive TV contract. Still, I can always dream.

☐ I don't want to watch second class Rugby. I'm a Rugby League supporter and I want to see the best standard possible. I think merging local clubs is a good idea, because the money would be channelled into clubs in one geographical area. This would create a big enough audience to support one Super League side that could compete with the best. Whether we like it or not it will come, so we might as well join now. Look at the Super League this year, it is filled with the dominant teams from the areas of the proposed merger clubs. The secondary teams from those areas are losing players left right and centre. I believe in centres of excellence. My other sport is athletics and years ago I was proposing that in schools there should be one important school for track and field where children from all over the district could go, one important place for gymnastics and so on.

☐ My allegiance to our game is such that I view the world through Rugby League eyes. I believe you have to, if you really care for the game. For example, I hate the convention of cricket commentators to call one of the bowling ends at Headingley "the Football Stand end" and not "the Rugby League Stand end". Or I become really annoyed when in alphabetical lists, Rugby Union comes before Rugby League, such as on BBC Ceefax. In my experience, if you are not for Rugby League, you are usually against it. This explains, in part, why the game has not spread significantly at a professional level in Britain.

☐ Have you any idea what it is like working in property and reading *The Estates Gazette*, *Estate Times* and *Chartered Surveyor Weekly*?

All the top London surveying firms have England RU internationals on their staff. I use the word 'staff' loosely. Full colour spreads every other week advertise their 'in-house'

seven-a-side tournaments and friendlies. Then they have double page photo spreads of the said tournaments. Recently one publication introduced a nominally 'general' sporting page, which at least every other week is written by one of their in-house Union internationals or Fleet Street acolyte.

A few years ago a chartered surveyor in Crewe worked, strove and fought to put on a chartered surveyors' Rugby League game. The Royal Institution's own journal refused to mention the fixture in its columns. Protests to the editor bore no fruit. However, I have since had my revenge, negative though it may be. When one of their advertising salesmen rang my firm selling space, I took great delight in telling him I always avoid his publication on principle when placing my 'situations vacant' ads and I suggested he advise his editor to be a little more cautious who he offends.

In similar petty, but satisfying vein, when compiling a shortlist for a job, I was inundated with applications and was able to reject, without feeling guilty, a high profile captain of his local RU team. I need surveyors who will concentrate on their job, not their rugby. I enjoyed my little yellow sticker which added a simple red 'No' to his application.

Incidentally, the fixture was played within one hundred yards of Rugby League Headquarters at Chapeltown Road. The surveyors travelled from all corners of the country. Despite ample advance warning, no representative from League HQ managed to stagger the shortest of distances to put in even a token appearance - a small gesture of support would have meant a lot to those young blokes. I doubt that they have played as a team since.

☐ You will recall the short-lived British Aerospace satellite channel which featured games from the lower reaches of the RFL. One game was at Chorley. Several supporters were concerned that the club's image would not be helped by the small crowd normally evident. After much discussion their plan was that if everybody brought a friend, the crowd would double. Unable to persuade their friends to forsake the public house, a couple of the supporters bought life-size blow-up Frankenstein monsters, which they carried around the ground trying to ensure that there always seemed to be people in view of the cameras. I have often wondered if British Aerospace viewers found it strange that several of Chorley's inhabitants seemed to have bolts through their necks.

☐ Summer rugby is going to be a right laugh here at Headingley. The cricketers and rugby players use the same changing rooms, although I've heard they're putting some changing rooms in the proposed new stand. But still, there is the fixture problem. There is cricket here all the time in the Summer, they are going to have to be very careful planning the fixture list. Then there are the test matches. Sometimes we have had two test matches in a season here and we use the rugby pitch as car parking. One year it rained cats and dogs and all the cars got stuck in the mud, the pitch was a right state. It took us the rest of the summer to get it back in shape.

I don't think the summer idea will last. Rugby is a winter game, you need soft ground and a cool temperature, otherwise the players get knackered.

☐ At the beginning of my first scrap book, I have pasted in my first pay-packet. Losing pay of £1, for Dewsbury - six points (Vic Hey - two tries) to Batley's eleven, at Mount Pleasant. Alongside the packet I have a newspaper cutting advising that Martin Offiah has earned between two million and three million in his Rugby League career. Obviously Martin is an outstanding attacking winger, but I was leading try scorer for two seasons for my club, which headed the Rugby League tables and I gained thirteen medals.

Our usual pay for League games was £7 for a win and £4 a loss, less tax. There were no

contract payments to players. The rule was "no play, no pay." This caused hardships. The pay received was very low by today's standards, but was useful. We enjoyed playing the game of Rugby League too. Match pay with lesser clubs was poor and was reviewed each year. £2, £3 or £4 was common. Much of the money earned was spent on good food, to keep up strength.

I have no grudge against top players today receiving top money, as elite people in all walks of life usually receive top payments.

☐ Three days before the original Super League proposals were announced, I wrote this letter to the *Rugby League Express*.

"I woke up this morning having had a wonderful dream last night. Today I am travelling to see my team - Pontefract Panthers - playing the Cumbrian Crusaders in the Rugby League Challenge Cup Final.

Last Sunday I saw my team win the League title by beating Humberside Hawks - at our new stadium in Pontefract Park - by 26 points to 14. It was a wonderful game watched by 15,000 seated fans who not only enjoyed the game but the pre-match entertainment as well.

At last we can now start to bury the old stigma of them and us, Cas and Fev, and rejoice in having a superb local professional Rugby League team, which is run at a professional level by full time marketing and administrative staff.

So to the day ahead, can we do the double at Wembley. As today's date is 3 October 2005, you will realise that Rugby League has changed to Summer sport."

I beat Murdoch and Lindsay by three days but I can't prove it, I didn't send the letter.

☐ It was the Duke of Edinburgh who saved Featherstone Rovers. I'll tell you how. For me, as a Rovers' fan living in Liverpool, April 1995 was a difficult month. University in the seventies and subsequent unemployment had brought me to Liverpool, but had done nothing to extinguish my passion for Fev. I'd learnt to stand on the Kop and admire Keegan. Dalglish and Rush, but still my dreams were of Mick Smith, bobbing and weaving to beat six men and score under the posts against Bradford Northern at Wembley in 1973, or Steve Quinn's last gasp penalty to beat the mighty Hull in 1983. All trips home to my parents are timed to coincide with a home game.

There'd been rumours in the press for a few days, mutterings of a Super League, but I'd heard it all before. Then one morning, there it was in black and white, ridiculous mergers all over the place, but the most ridiculous of all - Feath to merge with Cas and Wakefield. Utter devastation. Not since times of war had father

and son been brought so close as daily phone calls tracked the latest developments. Wakefield's directors voted in favour of merger, but Feath and Cas were vehemently opposed. With biblical irony, Feath played Cas on Good Friday. Never had this match had so much emotional significance. Cas won, but we all registered our disgust at any merger.

For the last four years I'd joined my dad in a strange ritual known as 'The Stupid Northerners' Trip Out To London'. A wonderful day out and every year the same itinerary.

6.30 am. Dad gets first train from Doncaster. I get first train from Liverpool.

11.00 am. Meet outside National Gallery. Also meet Dad's brother and cousins who live 'down south'. Look at paintings, usually Picasso and French impressionists.

12.00 noon. Go to pub near Leicester Square, drink loads, eat loads, talk about our year's activities, discuss match.

1.15 pm. Head for Wembley.

2.30 pm. Watch Wigan win cup.

5.00 pm. Go to pub near Piccadilly Circus.

7.00 pm. Dash to catch respective trains back north.

Dad has seen every Final since 1966, but I'd only joined him for Feath's occasional visits, until recently. Every year we had the same seats, virtually on the Wigan bench, just by the aisle as they come down with the Cup. This year it occurred to us that this might be an ideal place for some kind of protest, a banner. I'd never made a banner before, but I now have nothing but admiration for the banner makers of the world. So many decisions to make: type of material, colour, size and type of script and of course the message. I thought about "Send Murdoch Packering", but that didn't mention Feath. After much deliberation I settled for the hugely uninspiring "Feath say No to merger". It took three hours of Friday night to produce a large banner of third form technicality.

The day of the match and we meet on the steps of the National. We discuss the latest developments and then I unfurl the banner. Dad's impressed, but I know it's no Leonardo. After culture, alcohol and food, we arrive at our seats at Wembley. I decide to try a pre-match banner wave. Immediately six drunken Welshmen, up from the valleys, complain that they can't see the dancing girls on the pitch. They ask what's on the banner. They've never heard of Feath, but say how much they're looking forward to Super League rugby with their newly created Cardiff team. I explain that we've always had Super League rugby in Feath and that, actually, we'd quite like it to continue. I lean over the aisle and wave the banner towards the dignitaries in their box: Michael

Parkinson, Colin Welland, Brian Glover, Ian St John and somebody from *Eastenders*. Surely one of these has a bit of influence?

The teams come on to he pitch, accompanied by that dreadful Tina Turner song and begin to line up. I look over towards the dignitaries' box again and who should I see descending the stairs, but the object of much of my hatred, the man who, with Rupert Murdoch, plotted the destruction of my team, my history, the man who had belittled and virtually slandered Fev, Maurice (Wigan) Lindsay. I now know how Lee Harvey Oswald must have felt (if he'd done it) except I'm going to do it with words. I wave the banner and scream a variety of obscenities, such as,

"Have you had your lovely bonus yet, Maurice?" and other things a little less subtle. I actually make eye contact with him from a distance of about fifteen yards and I'm aware of somebody in front of him walking towards me and peering to read my banner and I suddenly realise that it's the Duke of Edinburgh! He reads it, looks at me, smiles and goes back and rejoins Maurice.

And that's it, that's how Feath were saved. As they walk onto the pitch I can imagine Maurice and the Duke's conversation.

Duke: "What's this business with Feath, Maurice?"

Maurice: "Not much really, your honour, just an insignificant former mining town with little to offer in our bold step forward."

Duke: "But didn't they win the cup in 1967, 1973 and 1983, didn't they get to the semi-finals this year, haven't they produced some fine international players in the last twenty years, aren't they, per head of population, the best supported team in the whole of the British Isles, and didn't that dreadful Thatcher woman have all their mines closed down? Surely, Maurice, they should be allowed to exist."

Maurice: "I think you might be right, your honour."

And that's how it happened. On Monday it was announced that all enforced mergers were off, all thanks to my audience with the Duke.

Never Been The Same Since The Dutchman Left
Developing The Game

☐ People stereotype Oxbridge Rugby League as public-school Hooray Henrys meeting up with the flat-cap-and-whippet brigade. It has always been rather irritating. There has certainly been some publicity mileage in it - not least when the then Great Britain coach, Maurice Bamford, visited Oxford as guest coach, and the photograph of him wearing gown, mortar-board

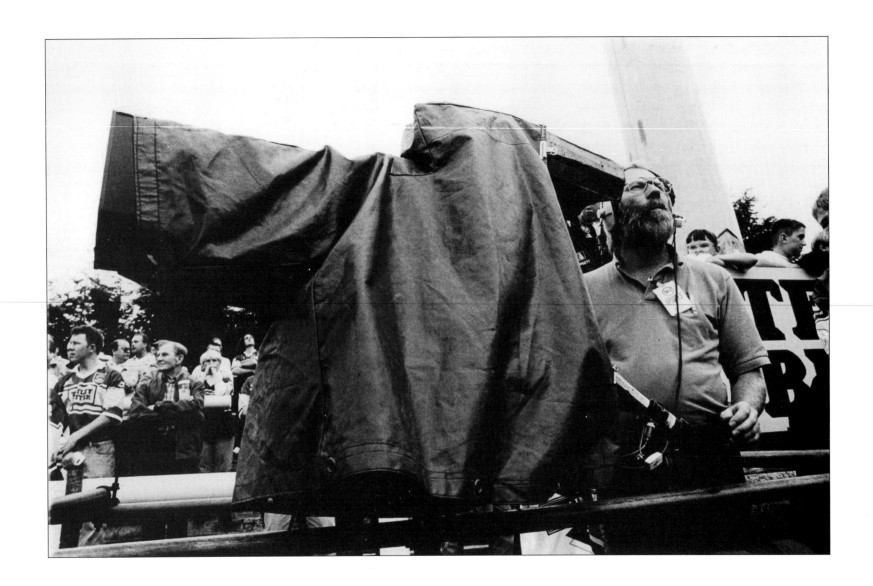

and half-moon glasses adorned the next day's *Daily Mail* sports pages. But most of the time it has just been an incitement for visiting teams to come and kick the crap out of the yah-boys.

In my experience, the Rugby League teams of the two ancient universities have been driven by exactly the same dynamics as the pub teams in the lowest divisions of the Yorkshire League. There have been hard men, quiet men and village idiots; banter about girlfriends, injuries, relative abilities, and who can drink most. The fact that there's the odd Old Carthusian doing the story-telling is neither here nor there, because there are no social boundaries once you get near a Rugby League field. The prince gets whacked the same as the pauper.

That's not to say that there hasn't been the occasional cultural interface encountered along the way. The same Maurice Bamford was explaining to the squad the difference in a defensive line between those would-be tacklers who were cocked and eager for the task - "dogs of war", and those who were relaxing or hiding - "bags of shite". It just happened to be an Old Harrovian who saw this as a ripe opportunity for japes, albeit not necessarily at the coach's expense. I shall never forget the expression on his face when Maurice told him to fuck off and stand in the corner of the field like a naughty schoolboy until he was ready to take it seriously.

I don't think that sort of thing happens at Harrow.

Similarly, one year we drove up to Leeds for the Varsity match - which was then held on the second Tuesday in March at Headingley, a couple of days early. We had been invited to Featherstone for a match against Hull KR. It was to be the first live professional match that many of the squad had seen and, although they had all heard of Featherstone (everybody's heard of Featherstone), not all of them knew where it was.

We travelled up in two mini-buses and of course, as the intellectual cream of the country, had ensured that everyone who could find their way to Featherstone was in just one of them. This meant that the other one eventually ground to a halt just outside of Purston Jaglin to ask directions from a local girl at a bus stop. The driver - blazer, club tie, brogues, impeccable home counties accent - leaned out and said, "Pardon me, but would you be so kind as to direct us to Featherstone."

She eyed him up, snorted, and said, "D'yer think I'm fucking thick?"

Nonplussed, he asked her what she meant.

"Yer in Fev," she replied, and stalked off.

Welcome to West Yorkshire.

When I started at Oxford, Rugby League was marginalised in the extreme, played only by a handful of ex-patriate northerners, their closest friends, and a few who fancied a soft half-Blue for turning out in the Varsity match. For most of the season, we'd struggle to raise a team until the third of these categories began to appear at training in February. Then we'd field a team full of novices against Cambridge and get stuffed.

What we tried to do thereafter was raise the profile of the game - educate people away from thinking that it was all about fat northerners with Ray French accents. We'd invite selected players to training, rather than pleading with them, as if it were a privilege for them to play with us. We'd send wildly exaggerated and dramatic match and news reports to the university paper, describing ourselves as 'Rugby League Correspondents' - and they'd print it too, being desperately short of copy. We upgraded the fixture list, excluding the likes of Fulham Travellers and including things like trial matches against Great Britain Students. We got hammered, of course, but it made people sit up and take notice - Oxford versus Great Britain.

And it worked. Rugby League became fashionable, this year's model, *the* niche sport to play. Rugby Union players who came to the university never having heard of the game were enticed into giving it a go. Some of them loved it and were hooked for life; some of them hated it and couldn't wait till they'd got their half-

Blue so that they could go back to leaning quietly on the side of the maul. The upward spiral we started has meant that Oxford are now recognised as one of the top five or six sides in the Student Rugby League and the sport has been acknowledged with full-Blue status inside the university. The implications of that are tremendous.

Why did I bother with it all? I don't really know. I've always had a yearning to work at the heart of Rugby League. When I was a teenager on the terraces at Trinity, and they sacked the coach (which they did pretty regularly), I used to write in and apply for the job. I suppose it has a lot to do with caring about the game so much, recognising the failings that have limited its horizons to date, and wanting to make sure it fulfils its potential. And, after all, if you want a job doing well, do it yourself.

☐ I should say the Keighley Ladybirds were one of the first women's teams and with the resurgence of the Cougars, the Cats have been encouraged. We look up to people like Julie Cronin at York, she's been there since the start and she's still awesome. Then there's Brenda Dobek, she could easily play in a men's team.

☐ The first season at Craven Cottage quickly established many of the players as heroes to the crowd. One of the favourites was Ian van Bellen. The sight of this determined man, with a large stomach, running straight into the opposition, was a great introduction to Rugby League for Londoners. He was allowed to leave the club after the first season and was much missed. Watching the team go down to another First Division defeat in the next season, we were talking to an elderly couple. "It hasn't been the same since the Dutchman left", they said. Somewhat bemused, we realised they meant Ian van Bellen.

Fulham Football Club had a great tradition in the 1960s of narrow escapes from relegation, often including beating the top teams. The Rugby League team tried to follow this. A memorable triumph in the second season was an 11-0 victory over champions-elect, Leigh. As Fulham fought to defend this precious lead, the tension grew - so much that the ball boys in front of the main stand got told off by the referee for time wasting!

The 1984 departure from Craven Cottage, and five of our players joining Reg Bowden at Warrington as 'free agents', left a bitter taste in the mouth. In 1985-6, we were drawn against Warrington in the John Player Trophy. Fortunately the bitterness did not spill into the pitch, with the Wire winning by a narrow seven points. During the game, at the Chiswick ground, a flock of geese flew over. One Fulham supporter's loud comment, "Sign 'em up, Bowden, they're free agents," summed up everyone's feelings.

Towards the end of that season, Paul Faires took over control of the club for a few months. His ideas to brighten up the game included linking the referee to a mobile microphone to explain decisions, disco music blaring out before the game and a fire-eater at half time. Unfortunately, he only managed to eat the fires on ten of the one hundred sticks he had lit and his performance continued well into the second half. The team became known as "The Bears", with *The Teddy Bears' Picnic* being played and *Another One Bites the Dust*, greeting the team's occasional tries. Fortunately, by the start of the new season, the club had new directors who dropped these ideas.

Dedicated supporters have followed the team up north on a regular basis, leaving London at 8.30am on a Sunday morning. Only occasionally have there been problems. Once a group of supporters spent the night in a broken down coach on Shap Fell, arriving back in London on Monday morning. In 1994, following a victory at Hunslet, the supporters' coach broke down. They were rescued by the team coach following behind, who picked them up from the side of the M1 and took them back to London.

Despite fifteen years of supporting Rugby League in London, some northerners still regard us as being from another planet. At Bramley in 1995, fed up with yet another 'soft southerner' comment, a London supporter stripped to the waist, despite a snow storm, and watched the second half of the match like this. He was defrosted in the bar afterwards.

Rugby League has been played at some unlikely venues in London. Crystal Palace National Sports Centre was 'home' for two periods. Overlooking the stadium is a small zoo. When support was at a low ebb, a rumour went round that the club were training the donkeys in the zoo to bray during the games to create some atmosphere.

The Polytechnic Stadium at Chiswick had poor facilities, but was our home for over five years. The stadium was rebuilt by the supporters in the summer of 1985, including manager Roy Lester using his welding skills to fix the tannoy system. Surely this is the only Rugby League ground with a model railway running behind the stand and a yachting marina across the road.

London is a big place and sometimes potential supporters have trouble finding out where we play. We were surprised to get a telephone call from someone who had supported the team on teletext, but did not know where we played and wanted to go to a game. He had got our number from *Open Rugby*, where there was an advert for our book about Rugby League in London.

☐ Rugby League and drama are the two loves in my life and to combine them in *Up 'n' Under* is a real privilege. I feel great pride representing my sport to southern audiences, showing the people down there what the game is about.

We have a dual task when performing this play, introducing Rugby League to theatre goers and theatre to Rugby League goers. You can always tell if there are rugby people in the audience - they laugh in different places.

☐ Any new directives to referees were often passed on at training sessions that were held on Monday nights, with the idea that they would be implemented immediately. The onus to find out what had happened would be on any referee unable to attend.

One cold and wet Thursday night at Tattersfield I was refereeing an 'A' team match, Doncaster versus Sheffield Eagles. The first half was uneventful and at the break we all made our way to the dressing rooms. One of the touch judges, a member of the same referees society as me, realised that I had been absent from training that week and informed me that there was now a purge on head high tackling. Any attack to the head was to be punished by immediate full dismissal, no harsh words, no sin-bins, just a red card.

The first half had been very quiet, but sods' Law, early in the second half, a Sheffield player tackled an opponent from behind and wrapped his forearms around his face. I had no option but to implement the new ruling, he had to go.

The Sheffield player shrugged his shoulders and agreed "OK, ten minutes ref,", and trotted off towards the bench. I called him back and corrected him, "No it's for good!"

"What do you mean, you're joking?"

"It's orders."

And off he went.

I'll spare the player's blushes by not naming him, but he was involved with the professional players association and a man whose opinion had been generally listened too within the game. Not a lot was said until the following week when the disciplinary hearing gave him a mammoth, unprecedented eight match ban.

The national press were full of it - 'Ludicrous interpetations, inexperienced referees etc'. I had five years' experience behind me at that time. Over the next few weeks, quite a few famous names were suspended for a number of matches and the game is now a safer place for players.

☐ Leeds Referees Society appealed for volunteers. Two of us came forward: Colin

Cooper, a retired Bramley forward, and myself, a young university student. I ran a few lines - once for Fred Lindop, then an up and coming referee - but the first big open age line I had was a tough clash between Burtons and Dewsbury Celtic. Early in the game there was a sickening thud; a great howl from the home spectators and I rushed on flagging vigorously. But in the excitement I clean forgot who I was going to report! What a relief when Mick Morris the referee stopped the game and said, "OK son, I've got him. Come here, ten!"

Another averted embarrassment happened when I started taking the whistle. I had an Under 17s at East End Park, Leeds, and had to borrow the home coach's watch when mine stopped. Two weeks later: same ground, same home team, and incredibly the watch stopped again! Clearly, it didn't like vigorous arm waving. To have a watch stop once was careless, but twice ... Just before panic set in, I suddenly saw the answer. Neville Hill engine depot in the distance carried a working clock on the shed wall. For the rest of the game, I pretended to look at the watch, but it was that distant building that really measured time.

Those contacts with the Leeds League were a great help when myself and friends played our first matches at Leeds University. I had tried to put on a game within the Chemistry Department,

but we just didn't have enough support for two teams. So the thirteen names I did collect joined as a team and that famous Leeds League Secretary, Aubrey Casewell, put us in contact with some emerging new Sunday teams. Our first opponents were General Accident and the enthusiasm generated by these late season friendlies inspired an application for official university recognition. The Head of Students' Union sport was a Judo champion and he handled all the silly Rugby Union objections with great skill. We had no other student opposition, so we put two teams in the hardened world of the Leeds & District Saturday and Sunday Leagues.

Cec Thompson was just about the hardest working student in the university, but we persuaded him to coach us, and his unique powers of persuasion convinced us we were world beaters! And occasionally we did win, through our totally unorthodox style of play. I guess nearly all new student teams have similar stories to tell and, like us, the initiative in forming the team would always come from the students themselves, no one else.

☐ Here at Leeds we feel we are as big a club as Leeds United. Big clubs need high profiles and that's partly the reason why I was appointed as the club's first full time public relations officer.

Rugby League's relationship with the media has never been a good one but if the clubs take time out to build up links with the journalists and feed them information on a regular basis, then they will soon see the rewards. I put out a newsletter to the media every week, *The Headingley Insight,* which is three or four pages of information straight from here. It includes interviews with players, the coach, feelings about the game, all the things reporters ring up and ask for anyway. If they need more information, they can ring up and speak to me. I don't know of any other club that provides such a service, but I'm sure if they did, the column inches given to Rugby League would grow accordingly. Journalists are just like you and me and if their job is made that bit easier for them, they know how to show their gratitude.

☐ Keighley Cougars have set an example on how to develop the game, the others should follow. The prime movers behind the Cougars' success, Mike O'Neil and Mike Smith, are from the terraces and therefore in touch with what the people want.

There is a tradition of community action in Keighley. In the 1950s, there were penny collections and all sorts of fundraising activities to buy the Lawkholme Lane ground off the Duke of Devonshire, in order to ensure the continuation of Rugby League in the town. But consequent directors have sold it off, bit by bit, to keep the wolves from the door and the club was run down, almost to the point of extinction, until O'Neil and Smith took over.

The Keighley Cougars name was not just some tasteless alliteration decreed from above. Mike Smith, a marketing executive, ran a competition for the name and a little kid picked it. Right from the beginning it was people involvement, and it has just grown from there. In 1986 I got a summer job trying to sell advertising board space to local traders. I didn't sell one. Now, ten years later, they are clamouring for it.

The ground is packed, the team is strong, the spirit is sky high. It is all a result of development with people, not ivory towered, we know best, instruction. Rugby League is supposed to be the peoples game after all.

☐ I went to watch Keighley play at Whitehaven. The rain was bouncing down and we lost badly, it was as if we hadn't even tried. I was cheesed off and thought, "If I couldn't do better than that." That night at home, I was thinking of ways how I could do something. I had seen this old hospital up for sale, I had an idea. Within eighteen months I'd bought it, got some builders in, converted it into a nursing home with 58 residents and sold it. I had to pay a lot of tax, but I came out of it with enough money to put some into the club.

I was introduced to Mike Smith by Tony Holindrake. Mike had been on the board of directors before, but he left disillusioned. We shared similar ideas, I told him I was ready to go for it and would he like to come along with me, and he did.

There was a lot of work to do. The facilities were poor, the ground was a disgrace and the announcer used to do me in, you couldn't hear what he was saying. We stopped the policy of buying old players and bought some decent ones. We did the ground up and put a bit of razzmatazz into the atmosphere. I'd been a DJ for ten years so I put that to some use and played loads of records at the match. Things started to pick up.

If you come down here now on a match-day, there are 5000 speccies all having a good time, watching first class rugby. We've got the best coach in the business, some great players, super supporters and a smashing atmosphere. What more could you want? A bit of stand up bingo at half-time is just an added bonus.

I was going to stand down as Chairman last year after we'd won the two trophies, to let some new blood take over and get a fresh injection of capital, then I could get back on the terraces, relax and enjoy watching what's going on. But the Super League block put an end to that. Once we get in there, then I'll probably stand down. You don't want to be hanging about when you're 62 and people shouting, "You miserable old bastard," as they walk past.

I'm proud of what has happened here. We love rugby and the crack, and it's credit to everybody down here for the success we've had. Five years ago nobody could spell Keighley, now we're getting letters from all over the world. I like things like that.

☐ As a coach you have to adapt to public demand, you cannot kid the people on the terraces. As a player, I was lucky enough to be associated with Leeds Rugby League club. I was a Wakefield lad playing in a team with blokes from all over the North of England, it was a very cosmopolitan team. That's what Leeds supporters expect, they want the big signings, there has to be a few stars because that' what Leeds Rugby Club is. Each club has its own identity within the game. I've coached teams at Hunslet, Batley, Leeds and Featherstone, and each of them have a different heritage and tradition. A good coach is aware of all these things and picks up on it.

Every club has its own stage. You can take an average player from the lower leagues and give

them a run out with Leeds and they will be brilliant, because it's the big stage and that's what suits them. Equally you can sign a top player and they might crumble under the pressure. It's all about adapting, you know what you have available to you, you know what the demands are, you adapt and get on with it.

☐ I have recently been on a coaching weekend organised by the Rugby League, which had John Kear talking about Video Statistics Analysis. They use this in Australia to look at an individual player's performance through digital taping of the game and computer analysis of their input into the match. This will greatly aid coaching and teams that have it will have the advantage, as video doesn't lie.

☐ Television is all about image. If you look at the people that do the expert commentary on Sky or BBC matches, they've always got slick, clean-cut accents and different catchphrases and plenty of flashy lifestyle. It's all image and they've got to fit that image or they don't get used. It saddens me. Don't get me wrong, I think it's good and I enjoy it, but you don't need to talk like that to know your Rugby League.

☐ Sky TV has put Rugby League into the minds of potential supporters outside the traditional northern homelands, but it doesn't always send the image that I'm sure some people would like it to. I was once chatting to a man from Brighton, who told me how he enjoyed tuning into the Rugby on Friday evenings and his favourite team was my team, Leeds. He was amazed that such a big glamorous club could have such a scruff for a coach. Dougie Laughton was coach at the time and I tried to explain to this guy that Dougie was a very smart man, and it would take someone with a high standard of dress to describe Dougie as a scruff. But this guy was adamant, "A bald-headed bloke with no teeth and a can of beer in his hand, he leads the team out before the match." That's when the penny dropped, he was talking about Adgi. Barry Adgi is the Leeds kitman, a traditional kitman in every sense of the word and he'd been walking down the tunnel with the players at the beginning of the match. Word got to Dougie and I never saw Adgi walk down the tunnel in a televised match again.

☐ The weather gods who make the north-east an inhospitable place in winter are doing their damnedest to stop the England versus France game at Gateshead. As we approach the international stadium, the rain and sleet drive horizontally towards us, the gale howls and the odd thunderbolt crackles. This is supposed to be a big night out for all the family but it's looking bad. We'd told everyone they'd have a great time and parents, sisters, brothers, grandparents and nephews believed us. One nephew is due to play Little League in the curtain-raiser - except the weather is threatening to stop the curtain going up.

We arrive early and go for a pint next door: there are a few Cas and Hull shirts, but most of the accents are local. Then we go, none too optimistically, to watch the stadium fill up. Despite the storm there are queues at the ticket booth in the car park. The east terrace, open to the weather's worst, is filling up with children in white plastic capes. In the main stand someone arrives looking hassled, but breaks into a broad grin and tells the stadium management, "There's a bloody great traffic queue on the Tyne Bridge, and it's yours!"

The Little Leaguers romp in the rain and the weather eases for the big match. To be honest, it isn't the best international ever and England scrape home 19-16. But the really great thing is that there are more than six thousand people in and they're nearly all local. In the bar afterwards everyone's happy and we know that the Greatest Game is a possibility now in the north-east.

☐ Wakefield had beaten Wigan. We were looking through the papers for the glorious

match reports and there was nothing. We were fed up, and over a few pints in the pub that night we decided to set up our own newspaper. That was early 1989.

Neither of us had much experience in this kind of thing, so we got people in to help us. Danny Smith of the *Wakefield Express* investigated the practicalities and made a lot of contacts - the *Barnsley Chronicle* looked promising for a while - until we eventually made contact with Tim Moat. Tim was into specialist newspapers, the *Greenkeepers Monthly* was one that he worked on. He was a good designer, could work an Apple Mac and wanted to do his own newspaper.

We launched the *Rugby League Express* in September 1990. They were hairy times. We did all the editorial work in the kitchen of Monarch Bathrooms store in Wakefield, seldom met our deadline of 10pm Sunday night, and ran with all copy through the streets to the offices of the *Wakefield Express* who printed it. We lost £40,000 in the first year and it was touch and go whether we'd keep going, but we plodded on optimistically and luckily we went from strength to strength.

The *Bradford Telegraph and Argus* gave us an office next to some printing presses which was a big help. The *Express Weekend* was launched in September 1993. The ironies of the paper's success are that, if the newspapers we originally moaned about, did cover Rugby League to the same extent that they covered soccer then we'd be knackered. Plus the objective to cover the glories of Wakefield Trinity in full has been denied, they haven't done anything since.

☐ It's simple really. I love Rugby League, my specialist field of work is electronic imaging, so I created the Rugby League Homepage on the World Wide Webb. Until fairly recently there was only one source of Rugby information on the Internet. This was a discussion group consisting of mainly Rugby Union fans who reckon the Vichy government had the right idea when they banned Rugby League. If you asked a question then you could realistically expect one right answer and twelve adverts for a Twickenham Kicking Jamboree.

This is what really made me set up the Rugby League presence on the World Wide Web. The initial idea was to give people from all over the world the chance to find out about Rugby League in their country. Not only that, but to let people do it without listening to Welsh Union fans blaming all their problems on Doug Laughton and his chequebook.

The site contains a results service from games played all over the world, specific interest topics and a sounding board for people's opinions. The difficulty in gettting hold of results and match reports when you are outside the north of England is legendary, but now, regardless of where people are in the world, with a computer, a modem and a phone, they can look up all the latest information on the Homepage. We have thousands of readers per month, a surprisingly large percentage of which are from North America.

☐ We had a really nice lady who did the typesetting for our match programme. She didn't have a clue about rugby though. I once gave her an article to type about the former St Helens player, Dave Tanner. It said, "While at St Helens, Dave shared kicking duties with Paul Loughlin." It went into the programme as, "While at St Helens, Dave shared kitchen duties with Paul Loughlin."

☐ At my club we have had a lot of Tongan players over the last few years. One of these Tongans arrived here on his own, having left his pregnant wife back home. A year later he had not returned to Tonga and it was time to renegotiate his contract. The directors asked him if he did not want to go home to see his wife and baby. He simply replied, "In my country a man can have many wives, but only one rugby career!"

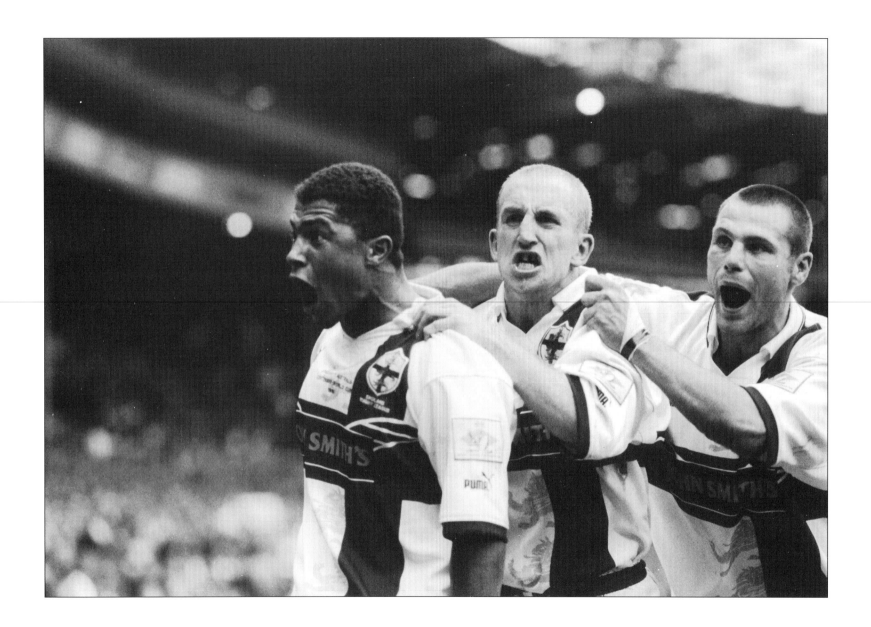

Later I went round to interview one of the Tongans for the match programme. He was staying with the club coach who had to act as interpreter. While we were talking in the sitting room, there suddenly wafted in an incredible smell from the kitchen next door. The door was open and I could see the coach's wife standing over the cooker stirring a huge pan. I remember she had a fag drooping from her mouth. I asked the coach, "What are you having for tea then?" He gave me a funny look and said, "Chuffing octopus, again!"

Going To Matches With Their Mams And Dads
Past Versus Present

□ Whitehaven may just be the most environmentally unfriendly team in professional sport. Sponsored by BNFL, NIREX and Albright & Wilson Chemicals, Haven's financial lifelines are inextricably linked to the economic dependence of the town on its Quatermass-like industrial plants. Such a reliance and the isolated nature of Cumbria's atomic coastline, breeds within Haven fans a unique sense of difference and independence from the traditional Rugby League heartlands of the M62 corridor.

Sunday afternoons at the Recreation Ground provide the focal point for pent-up Cumbrian pride, paranoia and sheer bloody-mindedness. When the famous chocolate, blue and gold jerseys do battle, the intensity of their passion and commitment has few equals. The opponents on the pitch may be the 'southerners' of Lancashire or Yorkshire, but it could just as well be Greenpeace, Bono and U2. Without Sellafield, Whitehaven has only the spectre of the dole queue, but without Rugby League it has no spirit and no soul. It is the ultimate irony that the sport's governing body were prepared to consign Haven to a fate worse than nuclear de-commission. Whitehaven fans would rather jump into bed with Greenpeace, than merge with the hated jam-eating Super Leaguers of Workington.

□ Why do we still behave badly even when we're aware of it?

When my lad was nine years old, he played for a local team (not so local really, but that's another story - I'm resigned to being a taxi). Every Sunday morning, hail, rain or shine - rarely the latter, frequently the former - and always bitter cold, I trod the touchline vowing not to open my big mouth. Then I started.

"Move up IN A LINE!"
"Move up!"
"Oh, come on, TACKLE!"
"Run STRAIGHT!"
"Run!"
"Pass the BALL!"

Clearly none of that was working. How can you catch the ball when your hands are clutched tight within your sleeves?

You know the referee isn't biased and is doing his best. But is he? Why doesn't he penalise his own side like he's penalising yours? He must have seen that tackle! That was forward! Never mind allowing play to develop and flow. How are they going to learn what is right? What do you mean, 'enjoy' it? They're there to tackle, not to stand off and watch. I'm the watcher round here.

The coaches tell them all the tricks; the moving forward with arms outstretched after the ball is played to stop the marker tackling the dummy half. Unscrupulous coaches, when they are referees, have been known to pull play back fully fifty yards and quite deliberately award a penalty to the side in possession, just as they are about to score. I once saw that done throughout a match so blatantly, it was transparent and quite disgraceful.

Cup ties are the worst. I remember vividly shrieking at the referee because he didn't penalise a little lad for not playing the ball correctly and the subsequent move led to the crucial try which lost my side the game. The ref looked at me with utter, undisguised contempt.

I'd made an exhibition of myself and I cringe with embarrassment to this day as I recall the incident. But it was a cup tie. And he was wrong.

☐ When a young player signs his name at the bottom of a professional form, his life changes. There is a level of discipline required, not just on the pitch, but in all walks of life. It can come as a bit of a shock to some lads, and the first six months are the crucial ones.

I overheard Rocky Turner telling off a player when he was coach at Leeds. He said, "There is no such word as can't." I've adopted that. I've heard so many excuses from players when they don't come to training - cars broken down, wife's ill, working late and the rest - that I'm ready for them. If they are out in the sticks and can't get a lift or catch a bus, they should set off at lunchtime and walk it, if they have to put a few extra hours in at work, they should start earlier. They are professionals, they get paid and they have got to be there. There is no such word as can't.

I worry about some of the young lads starting out now. They don't eat, breathe and sleep the game like we used to. It's not their fault either, I blame society. When I started out, I daren't get injured because the physio's bench was in the first team dressing room. I had enough respect not to go in there. The problems nowadays start at school, by the time they come to us, the damage is already done.

I'm proud that I have sixty players under me here, ranging from sixteen year olds that play in the Academy up to Steve Molloy, the club captain. I know who their mams and dads are, their girlfriends, their wives and kids and I listen to their concerns and social problems, all to make them better rugby players. Coaching is all about man management. Every individual has something that motivates them, it might be money or just a pat on the back that keeps them going. In order to get the best out of your team, the best result on a Sunday, you have got to make time for them all and know what makes them tick. I love it.

☐ Aren't some supporters weird? I once went with some mates to Cardiff to watch Doncaster. We are Lancastrians and not Donny fans. We only went because we had never been to Cardiff and we like to visit new grounds. Doncaster were really rubbish in those days, so we stood in front of the stand and cheered for the Dons. Behind us in the stands were the real Doncaster fans - two elderly women and an old bloke. After a while the old bloke got out of his seat and came down towards us, telling us to shut up - we had no right to shout for Doncaster!

☐ Back in 1957 some people said the Leeds versus Whitehaven semi-final was a boring affair. Under the old RL rules the Cumbrians retained the ball for long periods in a vain effort to hang on to a one point lead. Boring? There were over forty-nine thousand spectators in Odsal's bowl that day and I don't believe a single person departed until the final blast from Norman Railton's whistle.

What a contrast then the 1995 Premiership Final and the exodus from Old Trafford so early after half time. So much for Mr Lindsay and his gang and their rule changes, which have turned the game into a circus to accommodate TV. People will soon get fed up watching semi-finals and finals with scores of fifty and sixty points and more, however brilliant the individual performers. People don't go to the circus every week or fortnight.

☐ I hear stories about days gone-by of players having a bit of banter with the referees, but it's not like that now. Not even the captain can speak to them. They need sorting out. I was sent-off for the first time in my life during a Premiership semi-final for dissent. The referee had awarded a try from what looked to me like a forward pass. I was frustrated and I had a little moan, next thing I was sent off. No warning or nothing. That can't be right. The public pay to watch Rugby, not referees, and a good referee is one that isn't seen, but in recent times they want to play up to the crowd.

☐ Everything revolves around Rugby League - holidays, work, even planning my children out of season to avoid missing a game. My memories are of standing in the park with rain pouring down my face, to welcome the team home after they were beaten by Warrington. Of the emotion on the steps at Wembley when we defeated Hull. And of standing on the field protesting against mergers, holding tight to my son and wondering if he would have a club to follow as he grew.

They wanted to call us Calder after a local river. The only river near here isn't really a river, just a beck and I used to cross it on my way to the ground, down the 'Jubilee Steps'. Most of the time it was just a muddy ditch with bricks and rubbish thrown in, but sometimes it would be overflowing and we would have to tip-toe through. A bit like Rovers who can sometimes be sluggish, but on occasions they really flow and those are the times that make it all worthwhile.

They have now built houses where the beck used to be and at times I thought that was to be the fate for our team. I hope I will be wrong, the flow must continue.

☐ There's a chance for everybody in women's rugby, all shapes and sizes. It fulfils my need to get fit without me embarrassing myself in front of skinny little things doing aerobics. I'm a big lass and that's it, there's nothing says I can't play sport. But once you've got over that hurdle you've to persuade the doubters that women's rugby is worth seeing, that it's not just tig-and-pass for pansies. By that I'm not trying to say I'm tough. If somebody started a fight with me on a Saturday night, I wouldn't have a clue what to do. But I know how to play rugby.

The reason is the same as the lads. We were brought up with it. Some kids have parents who are ballroom dancers, they go on to be ballroom dancers. I was brought up in the scratching shed at Lawkholme Lane - my brothers play, my sisters play. I always had a vision of being a full back because of Brian Jefferson. I ended up a prop.

☐ Props now just stand with their legs open, it's all a foregone conclusion, they don't have to fight for the ball. Even if it was their head, in my day we still used to fight for the ball. We had some right battles. My hooker was Milan Kosanovic and his habit was to come up to me before a game and say, "Who is it today, Les?" What he meant to say was who were we up against.

I might say, "Dennis Morgan and Dave Horn." They were tough buggers at Bramley.

He'd say, "Oh no! That's a head-butting competition then."

And we'd be butting and nipping, gouging and sticking our thumbs in each other's mouth. Anything to distract them. When Bridgey came hooking, he was that fast I used to have to hold him back, grip his shorts then let him go. If your opponent was a shorter man, you'd lie on him, get his head under your shoulder and wear him out. Some I would grip under their arm, get their flesh in my fingers.

John Burke was a ginger-haired lad, very fiery, I used to put my hand across his face and cover his eyes up. He'd panic and start swinging punches. Trevor Walker used to break my back, he'd be under me all the time. He was only short, but as wide as he was tall and he'd tow you to death. His speciality was a tackle called 'The Cumberland 'oik'. Doncaster had a full front row of wrestlers: Mally Kirk, Georgie Goodyear and Ted Heath. You should have heard them grunting and groaning when they got down, it was like all-in wrestling.

Now forwards are the same as three-quarters, they know who's going to get the ball, so they just bend their back, put their heads together and they're up again. The lads I played against and with were hard as nails, but emotional inside all

the same. When we went to Wembley Billy Harris cried all weekend, it got to him. And when Keith Mumby made his debut against us, I remember him being really upset because they'd lost ... and he'd played a brilliant game.

☐ I want my game back. I want the simple pleasure of watching a game of Rugby League uncluttered by nicknames, Super Leagues, Mike Stephenson and Eddie Hemmings and above all, I want my language back.

No more 'hits' instead of tackles and 'busts' in place of breaks. Spare me, please, anyone who cares to 'put his body on the line', scores under the 'black dot', takes a 'step' or heads off downfield from an 'intercept', and I will die a happy man come the day we talk of defeats instead of losses.

Is tradition so dead we should bury it? Is one hundred years of a game we all profess to love so much to be forgotten, only because someone just threw eighty-seven million quid at it? Rugby League was never the perfect game, but it wasn't so imperfect that we should betray a game that owes more to the people that created it, sustained it and supported it than almost any other I can think of.

Above all else, it was a sport born of the northern way of life and sheer bloody-mindedness that shaped it heart and soul. We used to take it to London once a year to show the southern softies what they were missing and if they wanted more they only had to jump in a car and drive two hundred miles up the M1 to find it.

It is something special. It is ours.

☐ 25th January 1976 was a miserable day with a raw north-west wind. That afternoon a small group huddled together for shelter in the lee of the tea hut at the back of the popular side stand at Tattersfield, Doncaster. We (fool)hardy souls were there to see the Dons play Halifax. The latter were going through what must have been one of the worst periods in their history, but for the Dons it was quite normal to be at the bottom of the Second Division. So far that season we had won two matches - against Huyton and Whitehaven - and we had lost sixteen!

Conditions for rugby football were poor that afternoon, although at that time neither team were exactly capable of sparkling football. Twenty years ago Tattersfield had a heavy pitch at the best of times and there had already been sleet and snow in the wind. When the match got underway it began to snow properly. The vast crowd (at least one hundred and fifty of us) huddled even more closely together in small groups. Where the pitch was not churned up, it became a white blanket, and the standard of the football became even more pedestrian than usual. At the end of the first half, by far the most entertaining thing on the pitch was the memorable sight of a piebald touch judge. The snow was driving down the ground from the scoreboard end and the poor bloke was literally white down one side and black down the other. It looked as though he had been sprayed with a can of shaving foam down his left side.

Not surprisingly the referee decided to call it a day and the match was abandoned. The pulsating nature of the first half was demonstrated by the scoreline: Doncaster 0, Halifax 0. We all went home early with nothing to look forward to, but the dreary prospect of work on Monday morning. But at least Dons had not lost again, and there were a lot more Sunday afternoons to look forward to before the end of the season. Perhaps they could beat Hunslet next week, or perhaps they could beat Halifax in the rearranged fixture! In the event, they lost 7-16, but at least they beat Barrow in the first round of the Challenge Cup that year.

Now, nearly twenty years later, Dons have had their moment of glory. They finally made it to the top flight and it killed the club. They were killed at least in part by the way in which big money now dominates the game of Rugby League. If it continues to be the ruling factor, it will probably kill the whole game, or at least it

will change it into something few of us would recognise as the game and the experience we have so loved.

Despite all the publicity, despite the TV exposure, and despite the big money, the question of the future of Rugby League is a question of culture and not just a question of exposure and finance. The heart and soul of the game does not now lie at Central Park or Headingley, but it is still to be found at Mount Pleasant, at Watersheddings and Derwent Park, as it once was at Tattersfield.

What is more, I would much rather freeze on a snowy late January afternoon with a few real supporters, than have to buy a satellite dish to watch over-professionalised athletic prima donnas trying to play a winter game in the middle of summer, as they dance to the tune of an American Australian media megalomaniac who - as far as I can see - could not care less about the game and who knows and cares even less about the communities from which it springs.

☐ I only know a bit about rugby. How's that for an admission from someone who has stood on the terraces of Wheldon Road? They wouldn't let me play at school because I kept breaking my glasses. I do know a little bit about community. A lot of 'clever dicks' are trying to define what a community is, because after destroying so many, they have now recognised their value and are trying to rebuild them. Well, being a bit of a 'clever dick' myself, I shall offer some ideas of what I think community is.

A community is a group of people who know one another and have a recognisable identity that they are proud of; they are ready to act together for the common good and to help individuals who need help within the group. That help might be to the old, who have difficulty keeping warm in the winter, or to identifying a lad within the community who needs a quiet word in his ear before he gets into real trouble.

A number of large housing estates have in recent years had riots. There have been no riots on the Belle Isle Estate, and Belle Isle is one of the biggest council estates in the country. Belle Isle supports Hunslet Juniors, and Hunslet Juniors is one reason why there have been no riots, the kids are too busy doing other things and they have something to lose if they are caught.

Many rugby supporters can tell tales of going to matches with their mams and dads. I used to go watch Hunslet with my dad. Remember Hunslet? They were a great Rugby League side that played at Parkside. At Hunslet big money people were elected 'for the good of the game and the club'. They sold the club ground for a considerable sum and pocketed the cash. Hunslet floundered. Someone came along and offered big money to amalgamate the Widnes and Warrington clubs; fortunately the fans said something about that and it didn't happen. Anyone who thinks the closing of local clubs, identified with a community, is a good thing, remember Hunslet.

Rugby League clubs are an integral part of the structure that holds communities together. The next time you see pictures on your television of kids fire bombing a pub, remember that. Don't sit there, get yourself down to the park and support the young 'uns playing rugby, it stops them getting into trouble. I think Hunslet Juniors prove that.

☐ It gives a degree of satisfaction to see supporters returning home happy after a good match, this is a sure sign that the teams, management, police and other agencies have done a good job by creating a suitable, safe and happy environment for followers to enjoy their game of rugby league.

Directly or indirectly the Police play a very important part in the successful planning and running of many sporting events. Rugby League is no exception and police presence on match days is generally geared towards anticipated environment, pre-match intelligence, type of

match - cup, local derby or regular fixture and of course the estimated gate. Too few resources, and things can get out of control. Too large a police presence, and people feel threatened and the club rightly complains about the cost of policing the event!

The introduction of *The Safety at Sports Grounds Act* forms the basis of planning and safety in the partnership of supervision between the clubs, local authority, police and other statutory bodies. Regular liaison, meetings, and pre-match briefings now ensure that responsible parties understand their respective roles and hopefully this will go some way to reducing the sad loss of life which has previously occurred in crowded sports arenas.

During the season there are many amusing events both on and off the field. The 'characters' who play to the crowd, those who cannot control their emotions and burst into tirades of expletives at anything they disagree with - some occasionally running onto the pitch in various states of dress (or undress). There can be intense rivalry between partners, family or mates, often fuelled by an excess of emotion and alcohol. There is the stray dog which unaccountably gets onto the field to chase the players and ball, also guest appearances of figures like Mr Blobby who bounces around the crowd in an inflated mood!

Generally, the more people enjoy the game the less the police need to be involved. The benefit of rugby followers is that many of them stand no nonsense and often deal with potential trouble makers before they come to official notice - and long may this be so. More serious incidents tend to be policed firmly, and generally the relationship between spectators and the police is good. It is also a fact that many police officers are also rugby players, and supporters themselves. However, there is always the unexpected and a wrong or doubtful referee's decision at a crucial point of an important game can soon change a relaxed atmosphere into one charged with tension and potential for sporadic disorder and violence.

Reaction to other wider issues can also create difficulties which need to be resolved by local liaison with supporters and club management. A recent example was the holding of local parades before games, and demonstrations on the field at half time which were instigated by the suggestion of a Super League. More common occurrences relate to verbal abuse, invasion of the pitch, throwing of missiles or attempting to assault the referee and players as they exit through the tunnel.

There can be traffic obstructions, criminal damage within or around the ground, injuries or threats to home or away supporters and damage caused to vehicles as visitors leave. These and other matters all require continued attention.

A good police commander and his officers will read the situation and quickly diffuse potential problems before they arise. When push comes to shove the police are invariably close on hand to ensure the safety of those trying to follow their favourite team. Future policy is to encourage clubs to 'police' themselves and if spectators and the authorities work together it will benefit all concerned. Gone are the days when poorly trained and ill equipped stewards only went along to watch the match. They are now better equipped and trained to observe, read crowd behaviour and quickly open the gates in an emergency.

☐ As I walked through the door of the neat little grocer's shop in London's Notting Hill, I heard it. It may sound coincidental that the first team destined for the chop should in fact be my own, but that's how it happened.

"...ston Rovers will merge with Hull FC ..." (There have of course always been those who felt that the city's two big historic clubs should link up to form one big unhistoric club.) I just sort of stuck to the doorstep. I didn't go in, but pretended to focus on a tin of something or other straight ahead. From within, the *Five Live Sportsflash* continued its amazing scoop. I admit being selfish in thinking that nothing could possibly be worse than what I'd already heard.

So it's goodbye Cas, Fev and Trinity, hello Calder. Off you pop Warrington, Widnes, Oldham, Salford, you're all far too alike anyway. And Cumbria - ah, dear old outpost of the frozen north-west, well we'd love awfully to expand the game and all that, but not in your particular neck of the woods. Go play in the sea.

I didn't really care who was looking on, I just wanted to weep. But sheer bloody anger wouldn't let me. Excluding friend and family crises, this was the worst day of my life. From the people who brought you, "It's two, no three, oh go on then, two divisions," and the Rugby League scrum, we now had this. The people's game? One hundred years' celebration? One hundred? It'd taken just that many hours to sign the game's future away!

There followed something more about club chairmen applauding themselves (as chimps do), mind-boggling amounts of money, and mouth-watering contests where no one could expect to lose, but by then I'd had enough.

Back at my brother's flat, I sat down and copied the penultimate entry in *When Push Comes to Shove* into my diary, the one that says, "A curse on anyone who wants to make Rugby League a national institution at the expense of the small communities in which it flourishes." I

then packed my things and drove back to east Hull to help save my club in any way I could.

A Last Minute Switch To Carcassone
The International Arena

☐ I don't suppose Vienna will ever rate high on Rugby League's horizons, but that's where we met. He was a solicitor from Cardiff, a double-debenture holder at what they used to call the Arms Park and a lover of rugby, pure and simple. A conversation sprang up over a few late-night beers. He proved to be a genuine student of the Welsh connection, having followed the careers of most exiles from Billy Boston and John Freeman to David Watkins and John Bevan. His parting shot though, was deep, meaningful and delivered with suitable feeling.

"It's like my old headmaster used to tell me," he said, "there are two essentials in life, a quick heel in the loose and the Grace of God - in that order."

☐ Back in December 1989 I found myself working atop the Pyrenees without transport, when I noticed that the final Kiwi tour game was scheduled for Perpignan, three hours distant. After much coercion, a local motorbike freak agreed to run me there down the tortuous

mountain roads, as a time trial for him and without protective gear or helmet for me.

After powering through hours of incessant rain at breakneck speed, I thankfully dismounted among the Christmas shoppers in Perpignan as the boy racer roared off. Walking to the ground the total absence of crowd gave me an uneasy feeling. Finally someone put me out of my misery. Yes, a water-logged pitch had caused a last minute switch to Carcassonne. Too far. Stranded. Never again!

Time helps the memory forget. Jacques Fouroux's summer Super League rekindled interest. Final in Paris - very civilised. Through the Channel Tunnel, booked a non-returnable fare, but a bargain. Then what? A late change of venue to Narbonne, then another to - aaargh - Carcassonne! No chance! Stung again! French Rugby League - sans pareil!

One day soon I'll be going for the hat-trick - probably Carcassonne too. Vive la France!

☐ St Helens advertised for new players by putting an advert in the papers which invited "anybody who wants to have a go at rugby" to report for training. That would be in the fifties. Cliff Watson turned up, he came from Cornwall or somewhere, and he took to the game straightaway. He ended up an international. He became a good mate of mine, he was a tough

opponent and a great team mate when we played together for England.

We once played in France. Sergeant Major Clay was refereeing, everybody knows what a stickler he was. All the lads had him off, mimicking him, "Yes Mr Clay, no Mr Clay, no I won't do it again Mr Clay." This big French prop fetched Cliff a beauty on the jaw. Cliff wasn't half going to give him one back, when Clay jumped in.

"Cliff, not now Cliff, I'll tell you when."

The next scrum went down, the French stand-off was encroaching, Clay turns round and at the same time as waving him back, says, "Right Cliff, now."

While Clay's back was turned Cliff landed one on the French ten. Laid him out. Clay called Cliff over of course, wagged his finger at him and said, "That's the way to do it, Cliff. Keep thi mouth shut and you'll always get your chance later on."

☐ It is every schoolboy's dream to represent their country and it's the greatest honour for me everytime I pull on my Country's shirt. The greatest moment in my Rugby League career, and my worst, both occurred on Great Britain tours.

The worst was the famous tear gas test match in Goroka, Papua New Guinea. Papua New Guinea is a very intimidating place. When we arrived we were told not to go out on the streets alone. The people are very passionate about the game and they all try to cram in to their small grounds. For the Goroka test match, they couldn't fit them all in and they started fighting amongst themselves. The game was stopped and the police started firing tear gas at them. We just stood there terrified, I was shaking. The game restarted, and we lost to them for the first time ever. I wouldn't recommend that experience to anyone.

My greatest Rugby League moment was when I captained my country to victory in the second test in Melbourne in 1992. We had lost the first test, but had shown promise, and about 10,000 British fans had arrived in high spirits full of expectation. It was incredible, there were Union Jacks everywhere. The pre-match talk in the dressing room was all about not letting these people down and by the time we got back in there at half-time, we couldn't believe we were 22-0 up. There was silence, nobody knew what to say. We knew we had to keep our composure as they were going to throw everything at us. We went out and won the second half as well. It was euphoria, the streets of Melbourne were covered in red, blue and white. It was an unbelievable experience. I bet there was some beer drunk that night. We went back to the hotel, had a glass of champagne and went to bed, exhausted.

☐ I've travelled the world extensively and ,being a Rugby League fan, I often think it's like being a missionary taking the good news of something you believe in passionately to others who have not yet heard.

To see kids in Papua New Guinea playing the game on the local green as naturally as if they were in Wigan, or to see a grand final at the Sydney Cricket Ground, or to see township youngsters under Dave Southern's guidance playing the game with absolute delight, is a thrill that takes some beating.

I've missed the last two Wembley finals, but the BBC World Service is essential listening, especially when you're a Wigan supporter. I was in South Africa on both occasions and people there certainly know about the game and have great hopes for it there. Strolling on a beach in Cape Town, I saw a young man wearing what looked like a Sydney Bulldogs shirt; when I got chatting I discovered he wasn't an Aussie, nor was he from Wigan, but from Johannesburg and it was the shirt of his Rugby League team.

At an international meeting in West Africa, the Western Samoan Ambassador from Brussels saw me reading the *Rugby Leaguer* with Inga's photo on the front. It turned out he played

League in New Zealand and so the *Leaguer* went to him, then to the Ambassadors from Fiji, Papua New Guinea and Tonga.

☐ I went to Bangladesh on Government business. Normally when I'm far away I'm lucky enough to have a northern or Rugby League supporting MP with me, so we can have our daily fix of the game through conversation, even if we're a long way from home. Occasionally I might end up with Gerald Kaufman or somebody and then I've no chance for League talk. In Bangladesh I had nobody to talk to. Then one day I happened to get talking to the Catering Manager of the hotel. I can't remember how it came up, but he told me he was a big Rugby League fan. He watched it regularly on Star TV, that's Murdoch's channel in Asia. I left him the copies of *Rugby Leaguer* and *Open Rugby* I'd taken with me, he was thrilled to bits. So was I.

☐ I am a Rugby League fan from a distance and can tell you how many games I have attended - precisely one. It was on a very pleasant October Sunday in 1989, Fulham versus Carlisle at a Polytechnic sports ground, and the home side won comfortably. I remember repeatedly observing that Carlisle's trainer must have been an ex-player who regretted retiring too soon, as he managed to be on the pitch for what seemed like the vast majority of the play. My friend persisted in comparing Fulham's enthusiastic mature female supporters to women knitting at the feet of Madame Guillotine, despite my frequent admonishments that this constituted blatant sexism.

Living in Northern Ireland is not terribly conducive to enjoying the thirteen-a-side game. I was forced to play Rugby Union at school, under a tormenting teacher, whose approach led me not even to watch a game of RU for at least a dozen years. The nadir of the relationship between the two codes for me came when BBC Northern Ireland ate into the coverage of the last Great Britain versus Australia World Cup Final, with a tour match between Ulster and the Wallabies. The discerning amongst us were promised highlights of the first half and the whole of the second half live. By the time the chat and replays from the Union match were wrapped up, we were 'treated' to only ten minutes of the titanic Wembley clash.

Recently there has been some significant effort to spread the thirteen-person sport in this island. A couple of years ago, some students - many of Irish ancestry, rather than born on the sod - got together to compete in an international tournament and went on to arrange the first-ever RL game in Belfast. There has even been a match between teams from my home town of Newtownards and the neighbouring town of Bangor. Unfortunately, I only learned about these games after the events. I did just manage to find out the time and venue for the recent Charity Shield in Dublin - despite virtually no media coverage in the run-up, but ultimately the Sunday railway timetable and the 1.30 pm kick-off for Sky TV were not awfully compatible.

Whether League takes off over here is an open question (with over five thousand at the Shield game, despite a major Gaelic Football counter-attraction, there has even been some speculation about an instant Dublin Super League team, a la Paris). My own experience is that there is a lot of interest in and appreciation of the game, despite the local media's almost total dearth of coverage.

☐ Possibly the best game for - and maybe of - Rugby League played this year was the Ireland versus Scotland International in Dublin. The combination of seasoned pros and amateurs together, players all who love the game. And that's what they are playing - for love of the game and their heritage. And it showed.

The pros in these teams - were they treated differently from the amateurs? Apparently not. A well seasoned Scottish International told me they paid their own way over and slept in dormitory-style accommodation. At least one of the sides individually funded their own shirts.

It was quite delightful after the game to hear green-shirted players from the Dublin Blues with the softest of lilting Irish accents discussing the match. To be truthful, they were inquiring where the bar was. I'm not sure how Irish Lee Child's accent is, but his green hair was easily the highlight of the weekend.

Those spectators who only turned up for the sideshow which followed missed the best rugby of the day. One consolation in that later game was the soft Irish accent on the public address who made the familiar names sound almost exotic. I suspect the prima donnas in the second game didn't stay in dormitories.

☐ I've seen some matches in my time, but the Fiji versus South Africa game in the Centenary World Cup takes some beating for sheer exhilaration. Big strong running, crunching tackles, dazzling ball handling, flashy jinks and a gloriously full stadium to boot. Rugby League was king and we were Fiji fanatics.

I'd decided to break away from the norm the week before the tournament started. I opted to support a team other than England. I needed a team that wasn't playing in London or Wales and didn't have any Wigan players in it. Fiji fitted in nicely and my favourite big guy, Joe

Nadiole, being in their squad was an added bonus.

I rolled into Cougar Park for our new team's glorious opening match. I dived into the nearest bar and sat down next to a group of Fijians who came over in the early sixties to play for teams like Rochdale and Blackpool. That sealed it, no more was I an England fan.

After the emphatic win over South Africa, I spent all the next day trying to find a Fijian flag. The best price I could get was £95. I liked Fiji, but not to bankruptcy. I tried the embassy, it was closed due to a national holiday, I tried the library to see if I could make one myself, they wouldn't deal with me unless I paid a long outstanding book fine. I never did get to physically wave a Fijian flag, but I was waving plenty metaphorically in spirit.

I was packed in with the thousands of English supporters squeezed into Central Park for the England versus Fiji match. A few of us were cheering Fiji but I don't think our words of encouragement reached the lads on the pitch, our pathetic shouting was drowned out by the thirty thousand patriotic English yells. Fiji didn't get a look in and the 46-0 scoreline was very disappointing, although it has to be said that from a Fijian standpoint, the refereeing decisions seemed to favour the English.

Fiji were effectively dumped out of the competition and would clearly not now win the World Cup. But all efforts were not in vain, the Fijians had won the hearts of three new loyal fans.

☐ I normally spend my Tuesdays differently. I was waiting with eager anticipation for the arrival onto the pitch, of the representative sides of Tonga and Papua New Guinea to compete in a game of Rugby League in the World Cup. I was in Hull, it was October and the air smelt of fish. If I was asleep and dreaming, my wandering imagination could never have constructed such an image of paradise.

My expectations were high, verging on hysterical. I heard a rumbling "Boom-ber-boom-ber-boom" sound. I laughed out loud in joy.

"Listen Lorne, they are playing drums."

Lorne had a little more self-control and pointed to a programme seller dragging his wooden stand like a wheelbarrow across the terracing, making a "Boom-ber-boom" sound. Still, there might be drums later.

The teams emerged, resplendent in their exotic strip, the Tongans waved their flag and the brass band belted out the national anthems. The five thousand crowd were silenced through curiosity. Then it was time for the war dance.

I'd heard that the Tongan dance had only just been written and, loosely translated, the title was

Die For Tonga. No shortage of commitment there then.

The game started where the war dance left off, the Tongans were far too strong for their opponents, who sadly didn't have a dance and I guessed were quickly beginning to regret it. The Tongans were keeping the ball alive like I've never seen before, on one occasion the ball must have gone through thirty pairs of hands before the tackle was finally made. The crowd gave a knowledgeable ovation to thank these South Sea Islanders for such a spectacle.

I learnt more about the nature of Rugby League that night, than ten seasons of domestic rugby could ever teach me. I've been to the Boulevard before and it's a lion's den of partisan finger-pointing and shouting and generally noisy behaviour on the calmest of days. But that night, everyone had come to watch Rugby League, nothing else. The referee's decisions were less contentious than at any other game I'd ever seen, the teams were never offside, there were few dirty tackles and the attacking play was accepted as being skilful rather than as a result of bad defence. The Tongans went in at half-time twenty points to nil in front, we all clapped.

The second half was back to some sort of normality. We wanted Papua New Guinea to catch up and we got behind them, roaring on their runs and celebrating their tackles. It worked, they clawed their way back into it. I realised the importance of favourites and heroes at rugby matches and when I could get my teeth into supporting somebody, my blood was pumping and I was out there with them again.

I found a hero. Papua were desperately short of a kicking game, whereas Tonga had it off to a fine art. The Papua full back, David Buko, was a very busy man and coped wonderfully, catching the bombs and clearing his line with great skill. He was my man. His late try, jinking and bursting his way over the line, brought the scores almost level. I cheered as if I had scored myself and mentally drafted a letter to my club Chairman recommending he sign this man.

The game ended in a finely balanced draw. The teams were happy, the crowd were happy and I had learnt a lot about the game and myself. If only all Tuesdays were like that.

☐ At half-time the scoreboard, lit from behind by the slow train to Knottingley, read "Tetley Bitter, Cook Islands 28 - USA 6." From the Main Stand came the sound of Polynesian drums, and on the field some men in kilts were getting their shoes damp as they posed for the cameras. It was round about this point that those residents of Post Office Road not attending the game simultaneously chucked seventeen shovels full of coal onto their collective fires. Bet Lynch was leaving *Coronation Street,* The Russians were coming and the ethereal smoke signals curling out of those chimney pots on that famous Featherstone terrace made a weird accompaniment to the drumming that carried around the ground and out over the fields to Pontefract Crematorium.

The quips and banter on the terraces was predictable. Walt Booth, ex-Featherstone Miners Welfare and roof tiler of this parish, on first hearing the drummers sighed loudly, "Well, it's like bloody Keighley." And later offered a bite of his hamburger to a dejected American Centre struggling with cramp.

The opening match of the Emerging Nations Cup was a brilliant celebration of cultural diversity. Neil Tunnicliffe and his team deserve a medal as big as a dustbin lid. The people of Featherstone didn't let them down, turning up in their thousands.

And just to prove a point, the nation with about 14,000 inhabitants hammered the one with 250 million, as a boost to the little guy.

I have learned the value of investing time and emotion in things I cannot control and of belonging to a community whose aspirations I share completely and uncritically.

Nick Hornby, Fever Pitch

AFTERWORD

Sport, Friendship and Camaraderie

In my view, from these distant shores, Volume I of *When Push Comes To Shove* came as close to capturing the true spirit of the game of Rugby League as any book ever has. Leafing through its pages you could smell the liniment, feel the buzz of excitement that goes through the crowd in the outer when something special is happening on the paddock on a cold afternoon. Rugby League's literature is growing - in both hemispheres - and I welcome that. But this book was unique in the way it tapped into the true heartbeat of the game. I am delighted that Volume II has now become a reality and pleased indeed to be part of it from afar - albeit in a small way - through these words.

Rugby League has been part of me for all my life. A bad bounce of the ball ended my own career a little earlier than I would have wished, but the injury I suffered all those years ago, on a playing field in Parkes, New South Wales, way back in April 1953, in no way deflected my love of the game. Instead of being a footballer for a few more years, I became a coach and then an official. I've been one ever since.

If my career in administration took me to loftier heights than perhaps I had ever anticipated, it never took me far from my real enjoyment; being at the game, experiencing the tremor of anticipation as the combatants run out, thrilling to the wonderful athleticism and courage of the warriors who have played our game in the long seasons past. As the great coach, Jack Gibson, once said, "Rugby League is about simple things. At its best, the game is beautifully simple, yet majestic in its speed and hardness." And there is nothing complex either about the peripheral things that surround it. A chat with some mates on the 'hill', a beer or two with friends in the glow of the after-match, the supreme thrill at being at the special places - Wembley, the Sydney Cricket Ground, the Melbourne Cricket Ground, Sydney Football Stadium, Headingley - for the big games. These are the enjoyments of the game that came to England in 1895 and to Australia in 1908.

In 1995, those basic values came to mean more than they ever had. The ruthless Pearl Harbor style raid by the Murdoch league in April changed Rugby League forever. It had nothing to do with the fundamental things I have mentioned above - the things that have made Rugby League the game it had become in the 1990s. This raid was solely about corporate ambition and pay television, sparked by ambitions, petty and otherwise, of individuals and of the giant conglomerate which attacked our game. It is timely indeed, as we fight on, fiercely determined to hold to what we had and to care for it, that a book such as this is with us again - to remind fans everywhere of what Rugby League is really all about.

I am delighted to see *When Push Comes to Shove Volume II* become a publishing reality. Its words and pictures conjure up timeless images of the way our game has been and, hopefully, will be again. The book will certainly hold pride of place amongst my collection, to be picked up, leafed through, savoured - an instant reminder of the ageless attraction of Rugby League Football. Our game remains the most truly egalitarian of all - catering for all sizes, colours, creeds and abilities- and available to people from every conceivable walk of life. There are no barriers in Rugby League, just the reality of a lovely, immensely demanding game, played for eighty minutes on a weekend afternoon, one capable of providing the most profound enjoyment and of triggering the sort of friendship and camaraderie that makes a life worthwhile.

Ken Arthurson, AM
Director General,
Rugby Football League International Board

List Of Plates

Subscribers

B Dawber, Wakefield

Mrs K Hilton, Huddersfield

David Lyons, London

Brian Collett, Bradford

R B Austin, Knaresborough

Colin A Lomas, Manchester

B Rennison, Pudsey

A L Hosking, Ilkley

Sheila Cannon, Bradford

Bernard Rowlin, Hull

Stan Allen, Birmingham

Michael Jackson, Swillington

R P Sephton, Preston

M Kelly, Northwich

A Shepherd, Loughborough

C Todd, Scunthorpe

M A Taylor, Wakefield

Alison Todd, Doncaster

Trevor Nelthorpe, Stockport

Ian Ward, Oldham

Peter Moir, Rickmansworth

Ian Jackson, Macclesfield

Bill Lythgoe, Wigan

D Guy, Newcastle-On-Tyne

Phil Brown, Wigan

Geoff Ellis, Stockport

Robert Jolley, Pontefract

David A Dickson, Stockport

T M Driver, Keighley

Daniel A McCann, Whitehaven

D N Wike, Blackburn

John Barnes, Manchester

Mike Ulyatt, Hull

Cassie Willescroft, Chorley

J R Lace, Pontefract

R M Young, Bristol

M Ferguson, Durham

Mrs C Wilde, Selby

S Priestley, Bradford

G Smith, Manchester

A Ronald, Shene

Tim Leleux, Wellingborough

C Hutchinson, Featherstone

Mick Griffiths, Wakefield

H George, Goole

Stephen Boothroyd, Leeds

Bill Riley, Hohne Camp, BFPO 30

Stephen Dean, St Leonards-on-Sea

J Richardson, Selby

J E Irving, Carlisle

Patricia Arthur, Birkenhead

George Scott, Pontefract

J G Bannerman, Milnrow

Tony Spurr, Huddersfield

Wendy Spurr, Huddersfield

Peter Lawrence, Ilkley

A M McGuire, Keighley

Rachel Van Riel, Pontefract

Martin Barrass, Hull

Brian Saxton, Clitheroe

Brian Platt, Batley

C E Moxon, Stonyhurst

Trevor Whitaker, Bradford

Andy Gosling, Stockport

D Goldthorp, Barnsley

Steve Hobson, Wakefield

R Jukes, Featherstone

Craig Henry, Halifax

D Woods, Upholland

John Etty, Fleetwood

Robin Surtees, Liverpool

R C Weatherhead, Rochdale

Terry Casey, Bolton

Bill Nelson, Cumbria

Derek Enright, Pontefract

Paul Schofield, Pontefract

Darren Gill, Wakefield

Edgar Thrall, Pontefract

Colin McGuigan, County Down

David Thompson, Australia

John Pollard, Leeds

Terry Kirk, Pontefract

Janet Jennings, Wakefield

Ray Connolly, Thornton-Cleveleys

Chris M J Wilson, Wigan

Stephen Gleeson, Holland

John Hanson, Salford

Richard Clarkson, Wakefield

Peter Lush, London

Len Garbutt, Castleford

Stuart Evans, York

D A Mitchell, Leeds

P W Reed, Henley-on-Thames

Rev John Wickstead, Skegness

W Bullough, Wakefield

Bill Wickstead, Skegness

David Bruce, Manchester

Andrew Fowler, Sheffield

Julie Fowler, Sheffield

Alison Millard, Pontefract

Alan Walker, Wakefield

Maureen Williams, Featherstone

Alan Tennant, Featherstone

Kevin Haney, Wigton

Mrs R E Taylor, Malton

Glen M Dwyer, Australia

Diane Connell, Castleford

Amanda Lovell, Castleford

Hilda Fletcher, Featherstone

Andy Gladwin, London

Brian Lewis, Pontefract

Jill Brown, Knottingley

Dave Wilders, Castleford

Phil Brennan, Greenwich

Tony Brennan, New York

Jim Walker, Hong Kong

Peter Elliot, Wakefield

Ian Clayton, Featherstone

Ian Daley, Sharlston

Natasha Krasauskas, Pontefract